PENGUIN BOOKS

PLAY HUNGRY

Pete Rose grew up in Cincinatti and went on to star for the hometown Reds and later the Philadelphia Phillies. He holds the all-time baseball records for the most hits in a career (4,256), most singles (3,215), most games played (3,562), most at bats (14,053), and most outs (10,328). Rose made his major league debut for the Reds in April 1963, a week before his twenty-second birthday, and he was forty-five when he made his last major league appearance in August 1986, also for the Reds. He appeared in seventeen different All-Star Games and played on three teams that won the World Series.

PLAY HUNGRY

THE MAKING OF A BASEBALL PLAYER

PETE ROSE

PENGUIN BOOKS

PENGUIN BOOKS
An imprint of Penguin Random House LLC
penguinrandomhouse.com

First published in the United States of America by Penguin Press,
an imprint of Penguin Random House LLC, 2019
Published in Penguin Books 2020

Copyright © 2019 by Pete Rose

ISBN 9780525558699 (paperback)

THE LIBRARY OF CONGRESS HAS CATALOGED THE HARDCOVER
EDITION AS FOLLOWS:
Names: Rose, Pete, 1941– author.
Title: Play hungry : the making of a baseball player / Pete Rose.
Description: New York : Penguin Press, 2019. | Includes index.
Identifiers: LCCN 2018056333 (print) | LCCN 2019003052 (ebook)
| ISBN 9780525558682 (ebook) | ISBN 9780525558675 (hardcover)
Subjects: LCSH: Rose, Pete, 1941– | Baseball players—
United States—Biography.
Classification: LCC GV865.R65 (ebook) |
LCC GV865.R65 A3 2019 (print) | DDC 796.357092 [B] —dc23
LC record available at https://lccn.loc.gov/2018056333

Book design by Daniel Lagin

I'd like to dedicate this book to all my fans out there.
They made it all possible for me, the way they treated me,
and they've stuck with me through thick and thin. Thank you.

CONTENTS

PART 3
BECOMING PETE ROSE

PART 4
LIFE AS BIG PETE

Thanks, Dad

My dad taught me that nothing mattered more than winning. He instilled that in me from when I was a scrawny little kid following him around from game to game watching him amaze everyone in Cincinnati as one of the greatest athletes—and winners—any of them had ever seen. Dad was scientific in his study of sports and his commitment to learning and doing everything you could to become a better competitor. He had no time for talk like the old Grantland Rice line "It's not whether you win or lose, it's how you play the game." That was for losers. You might be hurt. You might be having a bad day. But you always looked for a way to gain an edge and you were always focused on winning.

That's why no number means more to me than 1,972, which is the number of Major League Baseball games I played when my team won. That, by a long shot, is the most ever by any player. I loved everything about being an athlete, from practicing to getting ready for a game to playing the game, but most of all I loved competition and I loved winning. I love baseball now as much as I always did.

Nothing that has happened to me could ever change that, including being banned from baseball for life. Or having to accept that I screwed up my shot at the Hall of Fame—and if, despite everything, I do end up in the Hall one day, it will probably be after I've joined my dad and my mom and moved on from this world.

Listen, there are two things I'd change if I had my life to do over again. The first is I wouldn't have bet on baseball. Of course I'd love to have that one back, but there are no "do overs" in life. You know the other thing I'd change? I wish I could go back and grab the boy version of myself by the shoulders and give him a good shake—he wouldn't have minded that much, he was a tough kid—and persuade him somehow to try to be a better student. I just didn't like school. I liked sports, and I was raised to focus on sports. The only interest I had in school was trying to stay eligible so I could keep playing sports.

I'll be gone soon enough. Out of the game we call life. I'll leave behind quite a few records. I'll leave behind a legacy of someone who worked as hard at the game as anyone out there, and someone who was as fierce a competitor as anyone who played the game. Anything I ever accomplished grew out of trying to live up to the example of my dad, who was the one man in my life I ever idolized.

I loved Babe Ruth. I loved Jim Brown. But I idolized my dad. I know I didn't always set the best example. I've made my mistakes. But I was lucky in life, and I want to use this chance to show that I know how lucky I was. I was lucky because I had a dad who was there in my life to show me the way. This book is my way of thanking my dad, and reminding people that no relationships matter in life as much as the first ones you have, with your mother and father. Being there for people counts.

I heard my dad's voice somewhere in the back of my head every time I laced up my spikes and went out there to do battle. That was true when I was a kid playing with the other kids at Boldface Park, and it was true long after my dad had died, way too young, and I was out there battlin' Gibson or Marichal or Seaver. That was the ultimate secret to my success: I always played for my dad and for myself and for love of the game, which to me were all wrapped up together, those three. I played my ass off when I was a kid in Cincinnati and I played my ass off when I was an up-and-coming star at Crosley Field and I played my ass off when I'd moved on to other teams in other cities. I was never trying to impress anyone. I was just trying to live up to that fiery love of the game and of competition that my father passed on to me when I was just a runt of a kid wishing I could be like him. I played hard because that was what made me feel alive. That was what made me feel like myself. I played hard, harder than anyone, because that was what made me feel close to my dad, even years after we'd buried him.

PLAY HUNGRY

PART I

GROWING UP

CHAPTER I

Big Pete

I grew up in Cincinnati, Ohio, close enough to the Ohio River that one time my mother stood out on the front porch of the family house and fished in the river. If you took a look now at the view of the river from that porch, looking out beyond a steep slope my friends and I used to sled down in wintertime, you'd think I was pulling your leg, but my mom really did fish from that porch when she was a girl. I ain't gonna tell you anything in this book but the truth. What would be the point of setting down my story, for people to read long after I'm gone, if I'm not gonna stick with the truth?

I don't know if my mother caught anything fishing from the river. I don't know if the family fried up some fresh catfish and ate it for dinner that night. I just know Mom fished from our porch during the Great Flood of 1937, the worst natural disaster in the history of Cincinnati. Almost a quarter of the city was underwater.

My mother was born in that house, where I was born and raised. It wasn't fancy, and it wasn't big, but it was just fine for our family, two levels, with an attic and a basement. My mom and dad's bedroom was right up front, and I had a little bedroom in the back. I didn't have many chores. Sports were everything, and that's what my dad wanted me focused on. But back in those days, you heated your house with coal, so when we'd get a delivery of coal, I'd have to go outside next to the house and shovel that coal into the basement, even if it was snowing hard at the time. From there you'd load it into the furnace to heat the house. Coal dust was everywhere, but it got the job done. We lived through some cold winters in that house.

I had the best childhood growing up near the Ohio River. We'd run into the woods and lose hours getting up to whatever mischief we could. The woods started right past our house and just kept going up the hill, especially once you crossed over Hillside Avenue. You name it, we probably did it, like a bunch of little Dennis the Menaces always looking for a way to keep ourselves busy.

"You have to picture Pete as this bumpy little guy," sportswriter Big Bill Staubitz remembers from those days. "His family cut his hair—they didn't have fashion styling back then—and Pete's hair stuck straight up. He looked a little bit like a porcupine. He had a gap between his teeth, and he'd spit through it."

The best was when we would walk a mile up to the top of Anderson Ferry Road to old Elsaesser Farm, which had been a dairy farm since 1929. They had a couple hundred acres up there, easy. Besides cows, they also had these beautiful horses, which we'd ride anytime we could. We'd sneak in and hop on and ride bareback. Now that was fun! No one seemed to mind much.

Those were fast, beautiful horses, and I tell you, I don't know if I was ever as happy as I was back then, thirteen or fourteen years old, my legs clamped down on a beautiful brown horse, racing along those rolling hills. I never did think about it too much, but maybe my lifelong love of horses started right there on the old Elsaesser Farm. Since those times, they've sold off that land to develop and it's become Home-o-Rama back there.

I was born less than eight months before the Japanese launched a morning sneak attack on Pearl Harbor, bringing the United States into World War II. On the same day I was born, Franklin D. Roosevelt was throwing out the first pitch of the 1941 season. Even when I was a kid, the family used to talk about my birthday, April 14, 1941, being an infamous day. That was the same day that Abe Lincoln was shot by John Wilkes Booth at Ford's Theater in Washington, less than a week after Robert E. Lee surrendered. April 14 was also the day—actually the night—that the *Titanic* hit an iceberg, just before midnight, and sank less than three hours later, killing over 1,500 people. Having a birthday like that kind of gave me a feeling of "Here comes trouble," but I never minded that.

You hear a lot about young people growing up idolizing movie stars or singers. I don't know, maybe kids today idolize billionaire founders of tech companies. I grew up idolizing my dad. Isn't that how it should be? My dad was my idol in every sense of that word. Someone you look up to. Someone you admire. Someone you want to be like. Everything I ever wanted out of life started and ended with loving my dad, loving the example he set, and wanting to make him proud of me. As far back as I can remember, he was the one point of reference I had, and everything else rotated around him.

I believe if you're raised a certain way, you'll *be* a certain way. I was raised in a real aggressive home with a real aggressive dad. I can't say for sure if you're *born* aggressive or if being raised aggressive can make you aggressive and being raised timid can make you timid. I don't know. I think I got a lot of God-given talents in this life, like work ethic, desire, heart. I think those are God-given, just like hitting a baseball with power is a God-given talent. A great throwing arm is God-given. Great speed is God-given. To me, it's clear as day that having the kind of drive and work ethic where you want to bust your ass every day is God-given, too. It's God-given, but it takes being raised right to make that God-given talent come out.

I know that when you're a kid everything seems bigger than life, but I really did grow up seeing my father as larger than life. We would even see articles about him in the newspaper. The *Cincinnati Enquirer* had been writing about my dad since he was a lean kid boxing under the name "Pee Wee" Pete Sams, before his mother remarried. In 1929 he won a special 105-pound AAU Ohio state boxing title at the Freeman Avenue Armory. At one point he was a sparring partner for Freddie Miller, a southpaw featherweight from Cincinnati who was world champion in the 1930s.

When I was just a little kid, the *Cincinnati Enquirer* gave my dad a good spread, under a headline saying 19 YEARS A FOOTBALLER! That was the big headline, and then underneath was another, smaller one saying AND A DARN GOOD ONE, TOO!—PETE ROSE ALSO PLAYS BASKET-BALL AND BASEBALL. Below that was a picture of my dad looking confident and athletic. I was always proud that there was a strong physical resemblance there.

The article said, "Pete Rose, veteran of Cincinnati sandlots, thirty-five-year-old father of three children and halfback on twelve championship semipro teams since 1929, can tell you a little bit about football." My dad was quoted saying that he liked football best, basketball second—and then baseball. "Anyone can play baseball—not necessarily well—but anyone can play, since good condition is not a prerequisite of the game."

The article even explained how my dad "started his career with Riverside in the old Ohio Valley league in '29, and led the team to a title in 1931. . . . An all-around athlete, Rose keeps in shape by playing basketball with the Christ Church team and cavorts at third base for the Tresler Comets in the Buckeye League, where he sports a .300 batting average."

To me, just seeing my dad in action was like going to the picture show and seeing a movie, one that kept you in your seat, eyes glued to the screen, not wanting to miss anything. You don't talk back to the screen and I didn't ask my dad a lot of questions. Like, he had a big ol' scar on his chest that sliced right across where his other nipple would have been. He only had one. But I never asked my dad about that and I never asked anyone else.

Come to think of it, I never even asked my dad—or anyone in the family—why everyone called my dad Pete. His name was Harry Francis Rose. How do you get Pete out of Harry Francis Rose? Later on, I heard stories that people said he picked up the name Pete because he liked a horse with that name. I have no idea if that's true or that's made up. I reckon no one knows for sure at this point. It's just funny how it can never cross your mind to ask a simple question, and then sixty years later you're still thinking about it, still wondering why you didn't ask.

I was an exact replica of my dad. He was Big Pete and I was Little Pete. I looked just like him and I played sports just like him. The only difference between me and my dad was I had great vision and he didn't have good eyes. He worked as a bookkeeper at the Fifth-Third Union Trust downtown, straining his eyes to read small numbers. He'd always had trouble with his vision, but that never seemed to slow him down when he played semi-professional football in Cincinnati into his forties, becoming a local legend.

You think I'm exaggerating? Everyone exaggerates when they tell stories about their dad. But I've got the newspaper clippings to prove it. The *Cincinnati Enquirer* wrote about him again in November 1952, giving him a big spread under the headline FORTY-ONE-YEAR-OLD NOW IN 22ND YEAR OF SANDLOT FOOTBALL—HE BOXED, TOO!

That was some article. "He's forty-one years old, father of four, still can run 100 yards in 10.5 seconds and after twenty-two seasons in organized football he still lines up at right halfback every Sunday afternoon. Who is he? The only person in Cincinnati matching this description is popular Pete Rose . . . unquestionably the oldest gridder in the Greater Cincinnati area."

Lower down, the article talked about my dad's cheering section: "Only in his case this section is made up of his wife, LaVerne, and their four children, Caryl 16, Jacqueline 14, Pete Jr. 11, and David 4." That had to have been the first time my name appeared in a newspaper.

I was my dad's biggest fan, and I was with him all the time, watching whatever he did. He explained everything to me he could. I was the ball boy on the basketball team, the water boy on the football team, and the bat boy on the baseball team. I'd be out in the car before he was, every time, ready and waiting to go to the next sporting event. "They used to be known as Pete and Re-Pete," said my old coach, Red Grothaus. "Little Pete was always in the shadows."

As we drove, he'd talk to me about things I always needed to remember when I was playing ball myself. He said if you didn't play to win, every second you were out there, then what was the point?

Mostly my dad taught by example. Since his favorite sport was football, that had to be mine, too. At halftime of his football games, I'd be one of the kids who would go around with a big hat to collect money to pay for the referees and, if there was enough, the equipment. Those games were a big deal. There were thousands of people, and some of them would throw in some change or a buck or two. You didn't see many fivers. These were working people. But that hat would always end up full. Vern Aggie, the coach, would use what was left at the end of the year to buy the uniforms for the next season.

Sunday football in Cincinnati was a big deal. There were no football games on TV except the Cleveland Browns, and when my dad played football, it was big-time football. He was shifty, and got to be called Old Swivel Hips for his moves out there, but he was strong and would knock you right over. These guys were good football players. They played hard and took it seriously, but none of them took it quite as seriously as my dad.

I ain't going to spin any stories here, so just believe me when I tell you that one time my dad broke his hip in a football game and refused to come out. I was standing on the sideline, the water boy, not believing it. He dragged himself down the field, determined to make the tackle. Another time, he came off the field with a knot on his elbow as big as a baseball. The guy on the sideline took a handkerchief and wrapped it around there with some ice, and my dad went back into the game. The next play, he intercepted a pass and ran it seventy-five yards back for a touchdown. Swear to God.

I had the utmost respect for my dad because I saw him with my own eyes, week after week, always giving everything he had to practicing right and playing right. He was always on time. You could set your clock by that man. Every morning, his entire life, he caught the 8:15 bus just down the hill from our house, and every afternoon the 5:15 bus stopped at the same spot and he got off. He never took a day off from work and never missed a game.

I was so lucky that he played my whole childhood. He played football until he was forty-two. It was hard to play football in those days until you were forty-two, with no helmet on. He played alongside guys like Chuck Brinkman and Dud Zimmer, football and softball, friends of ours, and their sons and I grew up right near each other in Cincinnati and all went on to play big league baseball. Don Zimmer, Dud's son, was older than me, so seeing him make the big leagues and having that example made me even more of an eager beaver. We all thought Ed Brinkman was on his way, too, and we were right.

Most people remember Don Zimmer when he was with the New York Yankees as Joe Torre's bench coach, bald and pink and round-faced, but always alert. When the Red Sox and Yankees got into a famous bench-clearing brawl in Game 3 of the 2003 American League Championship Series, Zim was right in the thick of it, taking a run at Red Sox pitcher Pedro Martinez, who tossed him down to the ground in what Martinez later called the one moment in his career he regretted. And a good thing he does regret it, too—Zim was seventy-two years old at the time!

He was the first one out there because he always got pissed off about any pitcher throwing at a batter's head. That was something he took real, real personal. In 1953, Zim was on his way to a future as a big league star, batting .300 with twenty-three home runs for the Triple-A St. Paul Saints. One night in Columbus, Ohio, Zim was batting in the twilight and a curve ball struck him directly in the temple. He lost consciousness and didn't fully regain it for thirteen days. Doctors told him later he was lucky to be alive. He was seeing triple when he woke up and could not speak. He couldn't walk either. He lost close to fifty pounds. But he fought his way back and made it to the big leagues with the Brooklyn Dodgers. Then, in 1956, playing shortstop for the Dodgers, Zimmer was hit by a fastball from right-hander Hal Jeffcoat and ended up in the hospital with a fractured left cheekbone and concussion. He missed three months.

"My teammates later told me they were convinced Hal Jeffcoat was throwing at me, maybe in retaliation for [Gil] Hodges's homer," Zimmer said later. "I don't know. Only Jeffcoat does, and he never called me or sent me a card when I was in the hospital."

That's why Zimmer was so pissed off at Pedro Martinez. He was a little shook up when he was thrown down to the grass, but he was just fine. Zim was always tough, and he was like me in being brought up to see his dad as a larger-than-life figure who told him to give his all in sports all the time.

My dad played softball with Zim's dad, whose real name was Harold Zimmer, but everyone knew him as Dud. Everyone called him Dud except me. I called him Mr. Zimmer because I was always raised to be respectful to my elders. Dud Zimmer was in the produce business. He'd gone in with a partner, Bill Thornton, and opened Zimmer and Thornton Wholesale Fruit and Vegetables on Second Street in downtown Cincinnati, which was a fixture from the 1930s on.

I'd stop by there sometimes to talk baseball with Mr. Zimmer. He'd smile and shake my hand and we could talk for hours. If I had a question about baseball, or something that happened in one of my games, I could always ask Mr. Zimmer and he'd have a good answer for me. He might even have an apple for me, too, and those were always good apples. Or, since Mr. Zimmer and my dad played on the same softball team, I'd talk to him there. I didn't know anyone else who had a son in the big leagues, so I always liked talking to Mr. Zimmer.

Eddie Brinkman's dad was a better ballplayer than Don's dad, and Eddie was a better ballplayer than I was growing up. We were on the same team together, and he was the one who caught everyone's eye. Don Zimmer played in my Little League in Cincinnati, and played football and baseball at Western Hills High School, just like I did, for the same coaches, only he was ten years older than me. Don had a younger brother who was a really good ballplayer, too, Harold Jr., who we just called Junior, but Junior was kind of a hothead and never cracked the big leagues despite playing minor league ball. Don wasn't a hothead. He was a hell of a football player, a running back like me, and he played shortstop on the baseball team. Don wasn't big, but he was fast, and he was tough. We were all tough in those days. That was just how we were raised. Our dads were tough. And if your dad is tough, and you're an athlete, you're going to be tough.

The Brooklyn Dodgers signed Don Zimmer out of our high school in 1949 as a shortstop. When he started his pro career playing for the Cambridge Dodgers of the Eastern Shore League, it was big news in the neighborhood. We all kept tabs on his progress. By 1952 he'd risen to Double A, playing for the Mobile Bears, then the next year it was the St. Paul Saints. By 1954 Don was with the Brooklyn

Dodgers, managed by Walter Alston, playing alongside Duke Snider, Jackie Robinson, Roy Campanella, Gil Hodges, and Pee Wee Reese. To us that was about the most amazing thing ever, Dud Zimmer's son playing side by side with legends of the game.

We went to Crosley Field a lot. My dad would buy himself a ticket and then have me bum my own ticket. I guess I was always good at talking to people, and I don't remember it ever being that hard to get a ticket on my own.

I was five years old the first time my dad brought me out to Crosley Field. We sat in the unreserved seats out in right field. I was thrilled to be there, but I was mad about where we were sitting. I figured I'd never be able to catch a ball out there in right field. I was right. But later, when my dad landed seats near the dugout, I got lucky. I think for every kid, the proudest moment in your life is when you catch a foul pop at a baseball game. I caught mine on the bounce, but the point was: I caught it.

We never ate hot dogs at the baseball game or anything like that. Better to save up to buy a ticket again soon. We'd eat at home, then head over to the ballpark. My favorite player when I was little was Johnny Temple, the Reds' All-Star second baseman in the 1950s. I used to love watching him and Roy McMillan turn the double play, and I think I knew right then I was going to be a second baseman.

Any game was a good game to see, but we looked forward to having the Brooklyn Dodgers in town. Since those games were special, my dad would work it where he would get seats behind the dugout through his bank, so we were in the thick of the action, not up in the nosebleed seats. Before the game, we'd head out to the visitors' clubhouse, which at Crosley Field was in a separate building behind the stadium. My dad and I would hang around back there waiting for Don Zimmer to come out, and then Don would introduce us to Jackie and Duke and Pee Wee. Seriously, I'd be shaking their hands, and talking to Carl Erskine and Roy Campanella and Carl Furillo. I got to meet all those guys because I knew Don. That was unbelievable for me. I'm just a kid, thirteen, fourteen years old, and I'm getting to meet Jackie Robinson? I remember he was a real nice guy with a high-pitched voice. Then, after meeting some players pregame, I'd sit in the stands with my dad and watch them play. Jackie played as hard as anyone I ever saw. I guess he had to, since he was so scrutinized, with so many people second-guessing Walter O'Malley for taking a chance on him. Those Dodgers all played hard. My dad would be sitting next to me telling me to watch this guy's moves or watch that guy's moves. He'd always insist that I keep a close eye on Roy Campanella, the Dodger catcher, because at that age I was still a catcher. The only disappointment of those days was that I never got to see Don play. He was a backup to Pee Wee Reese and it seemed like Pee Wee never came out of the lineup.

We'd watch the Browns during football season on our fuzzy little eight-inch black-and-white, because that was the only pro football we could see. Baseball was even harder to make out on the small screen. I remember one time watching that little TV with my dad. It was the St. Louis Cardinals, and Enos "Country" Slaughter was up to bat. This would have been 1951 or 1952, so Slaughter was in his mid-thirties by then, but he worked a base on balls—and then took off running to first. I'd never seen that before. My dad was watching me study the action on the little TV.

"Did you see the way he got down to first?" my dad asked me, sounding serious.

I nodded.

"That's the way you're supposed to get to first," he told me, "because the faster you get there, the faster you're going to touch that home plate."

My dad didn't have to tell me twice. I got the point. From then on, I always ran to first base, every single time. It was actually kind of a funny story how Slaughter took to running so much himself. He was in the Cardinals' farm system, playing in Columbus, Georgia, in 1936, and always ran in from his spot in right field at the end of each inning, but then would slow down and walk the last few feet to the dugout.

"Son, if you're tired, I'll get some help," his manager told him.

That was Eddie Dyer, who managed the Cardinals to the World Series in 1946 and won. He knew just what to say to Enos Slaughter to light a fire under his ass.

"From 1936 until I finished my career, I never walked on a ball field," Slaughter told Donald Honig for his book *Baseball Between the Lines*. "I left the dugout running and I hit the top step running coming back. And I always ran out everything I hit."

That was me after that. I always ran out everything I hit and always ran to first base, every chance I had—and I never cared what anyone had to say about it, either. I had to be me. I had to play the way my dad brought me up to play. Why walk when you can run?

CHAPTER 2

Leland T. Jones's Leather Strap

From the time I was knee-high to a grasshopper, what trade did I have? Sports. It was always sports. I was destined to be an athlete. Maybe the only book I ever read cover to cover was the *Major League Baseball Rule Book*. When I was growing up, in the 1940s and '50s, everybody wasn't so conscientious about going to college. If I'd have been an A student, maybe I'd have liked school a little better, but if I'd have been an A student, I'd have been a whole different person. I tell people today: Get as much education as you possibly can. Don't be like me. I was lucky. It worked out OK for me, but what would have happened if I didn't have the talent I had for hitting? What would I be today? I'd be standing down on the corner holding up a sign: WILL WORK FOR FOOD.

I was the kind of kid the principal got to know real well. Our principal at Sayler Park Elementary School was an older gentleman named Leland T. Jones, and I was sent to see him more than anyone. I didn't blow anything up or hurt anyone or get in any serious trouble. I'd just be goofing off, making cracks in class, getting into the odd scuffle with the other boys. The next thing you knew, I'd be sitting there waiting to go in and see Mr. Leland T. Jones one more time.

"Grab your ankles!" he'd say.

He had a leather belt he'd use to whack my ass. I know what you're thinking. That he'd make me drop my pants and pound away until I had welts. But no, he wasn't savage or anything. He let me keep my jeans on. He'd just give me a couple whacks, which was more than enough to get my attention. That hurt like hell! When I look back on it now, all these years later, it seems kind of funny, but in those days it was scary. Other kids were called in there, and once was enough for them. After that, they made sure never to get in trouble so they could avoid being sent to Mr. Leland T. Jones's office ever again. I was different. I must have made five or six trips to that office and been whacked a good dozen times. I feel like I remember every whack to this day.

I think most of the teachers actually liked me pretty well. I may have been mischievous, an active kid with too much energy, but everyone knew I was an athlete. There were some teachers I got along real well with, like Wee Willie Hubbard, who taught geometry. Later on in life I'd break a famous record set by a player named Wee Willie Keeler. Wee Willie Hubbard was a great guy who stood about five foot three. I had no interest in geometry—I can't even spell "geometry" without a little help—but that was one class I kind of half enjoyed.

For homeroom I had Alice Darby, who was tall and thin with glasses and had a real small head, and also taught science. Alice Darby must have had a lot of patience. I just couldn't sit still. I had way too much energy. I took the bus to and from school every day, and it was forty-five minutes, with stops, but to me it felt like I was on there for hours. That's how much I hated being cooped up, and sitting in homeroom was even worse. Maybe sometimes I earned a visit to Leland T. Jones just for a change of scenery.

My family wasn't poor or anything like that. My dad never missed a day at the bank, and he provided for his family. We had money for the basics, for the things that we really needed, and not too much else. My dad was always bringing home tickets to sporting events—he could always find two bits when he needed it for a ticket—but in our family, it was my mother who handled the money, little that there was. That wasn't something we understood as kids, but I remember one time when I was five or six years old starting to figure that out.

My mother counted out enough money for my father to get a pair of shoes for my sister Jackie. He set off that morning like he always did, catching the 8:15 bus to work, and we knew he'd be back at 5:15, the way he always was. He came back up the little hill and walked in the front door, and my sister was there waiting for him. She couldn't wait to see her new shoes. That was a big deal, new shoes. My dad had a box in his hands and he tossed it over to me, not to my sister. I opened it up and guess what was inside? Boxing gloves.

I'll never forget the look on my mother's face. She was not happy.

"Where are Jackie's shoes?" she asked my dad.

"Shoes?" he asked. "She doesn't need shoes. It's summertime. This guy's got to learn how to defend hisself."

That was the only time I ever saw my mom mad at my dad. There was some tension in the house, I can remember that. The next day, my dad caught the morning bus just like always and came back at 5:15 with a pair of new shoes for Jackie.

I did some boxing as a kid. You were supposed to be sixteen to fight in the Cincinnati Golden Gloves competition, but I started fighting when I was fourteen and boxed in the 112-pound class. I took some poundings. One time I fought Candy Jamison, who was twenty years older than me. This was at the Findlay Street Neighborhood House. There were five hundred people at the fight, and the only white people were my mom and my dad and my trainer. Candy Jamison had five kids at ringside. Five fucking kids at ringside! He beat me, but he didn't knock me out.

Another time, in April 1957, I went against Virgil Cole, again at the Findlay Street Neighborhood House. Virgil knew how to fight, and he had an edge in both strength and experience. He'd work my body, then land a few punches on my face, then work my body some more. It was methodical. I knew soon enough that my main goal was to survive.

"Dad, can't you stop it?" my sister Caryl cried out. "They're beating his brains out. They're killing him."

My dad was never going to stop a fight of mine. A quitter could never win. That was the first rule of sports: You were in it until the end unless they had to carry you away, and I stayed on my feet the whole fight. Not that it was easy for my old man. He was a little shook up, watching me take that beating. Back home afterward, he was somber, seeing the welts and bruises all over me.

"Look at me," I was telling the family. "But he couldn't knock me out."

Those fights were a good learning experience for me. What I learned was I didn't want to be a fighter. Virgil and Candy were real fighters. I didn't know what I was doing. I was a wannabe.

I got up to two fights and then I said, "Dad, give me my baseball bat, I want to get rid of these boxing gloves."

I didn't have a future in boxing, but later on when it came time to scuffle, I always knew what I was doing, and that helped me. As my high school football teammate Jim Wietholter put it: "The inside dope on him was that if you got in a fight with him, you had better kill him because that was the only way he was going to quit." That was Jim exaggerating a little. I had a quick trigger, but I wasn't a hothead in the sense of losing sight of the bigger picture, which was winning, not taking yourself out of the game. I hated to lose.

If you hated to lose, you put more into preparation than anyone else. From the time I was a kid, I was always really good about practicing. My dad instilled in me a fire to make the most of every chance to get better. I never got tired of taking batting practice or taking grounds balls or playing pepper or anything else you did to make yourself a better baseball player. I had fun doing everything. Sometimes it was hard work, especially on a hot summer day in Cincinnati, but I didn't look at it as work.

To me it was preparation, and preparation was always sacred. I got that from watching my dad. If you practiced that way, your teammates were going to do it, too, and they were going to get better. You couldn't have goldbrickers. You needed guys out there working their asses off. I always worked my ass off, and that rubbed off on the other guys. It didn't get the job done when you had teammates treating practice like a honeymoon. You could get the honeymoon after you won.

My dad was always talking to me about how you had to focus on what mattered and tune out the rest. You were there to play, and there to win, and everything else was secondary. Of course you made friends with the guys on your team, but that was secondary, too. Mostly you focused on winning, and if you were winning, the friendships would be there. You cared about your teammates, you asked how they were doing, what was up with them, because if you understood each other better, you were going to do a better job of working together to win.

I always tried to get along with every teammate I ever had, and I never cared if they were from another country or spoke a different language or if their skin color was different from mine. Why would I have cared about any of that stuff? None of it had to do with winning, which was the only thing and the everything. My dad was the same way. He loved to compete and loved teammates who battled alongside him and never cared if they were black or white or purple.

I never heard my dad or anyone in my family say a bad thing about a black person. He didn't have a racist bone in his body. Neither did my mom. There were only three or four black families who lived in our area, whose kids went to school with us. Nowadays that area is pretty much all African American. It couldn't have been easy back then for those first families, moving into neighborhoods when they had to figure that not everybody wanted them. That was one reason we always did what we could to make them feel welcome. I was always friendly with the black kids I met in school or playing sports. It wasn't anything I worked at or ever thought about twice. It just came naturally to me.

Later on, when I was making a name for myself with the Cincinnati Reds, *Time* magazine did an article about me and called me

"Irish." I guess my family background is partly Irish, since so many Irish came to this country, and a lot of my ancestors were in this country going back to the time of the American Revolution. Mostly, I come from German stock. My mother's family was German. She was born LaVerne Bloebaum and had a grandfather who was born in Germany in 1832. But being German Irish or German English or whatever the heck I might be never helped me hit a baseball.

I never heard anything about my dad's dad. My dad's parents had split up and divorced. Back in the 1930s, that was something that a lot of times you just didn't talk about. My dad's mother, born Eva Kathryn Smart, got married again, moving in with a man named Harry Sams. My mom's dad, Mr. Bloebaum, died about two months before I was born, and I never met my mom's mom. The only real grandparent I ever met was Eva. I always looked at Harry Sams as my grandpa because he was married to my grandma.

I lived with my grandma for weeks at a time during the summers. I did that, like I did everything, because of sports. My family lived on the other side of the border for Little League Baseball, what we called Knothole Baseball in Cincinnati, and that meant we had to give them my grandma's address for me to play nearby. She lived right next to Boldface Park and could look out her back window and see us playing down on the baseball field. I would live with her and Harry Sams for a month or six weeks every summer and spend all my time down at Boldface Park playing baseball.

For some crazy reason, my grandma Eva had a pet monkey, a spider monkey she took to calling Pete. I think she named that thing for me. If you've never met a spider monkey, you might think they're cute and cuddly. Not my grandma's spider monkey, Pete. She had a big back room with the tallest walls in the world, and that monkey would always hide up there somewhere. That bastard was mean. He'd bite you and then scamper away. He was nasty, but my grandma loved him. Why would she buy a damn toy monkey like that?

Cincinnati was a baseball city, and we had a good team. If you grew up then where I did, you knew that Cincinnati was the real birthplace of baseball, the real breeding ground, not Cooperstown, which is just a story they tell. The Cincinnati Reds started out in 1869 as the Cincinnati Red Stockings, becoming the first professional baseball team in the country. They toured the country looking for other teams to play at a time when baseball wasn't a "field of dreams," but more of a rough-and-rowdy spectacle, like a fight you'd see spilling out of a saloon.

The Red Stockings traveled all the way out to California in 1869. As *The New York Times* reported from San Francisco that September 23, "The Cincinnati 'Red Stockings' reached Sacramento to-day, and will arrive in this city tonight. They will play the first game with the Eagle nine on Saturday." A follow-up dispatch a week or two later explained that the Red Stockings had "beat our local clubs badly" and would soon depart for home.

The following summer, the *Cincinnati Chronicle* published an article scolding the ballplayers for complaining about negative press articles when they started charging fifty cents for their games. "The Red Stockings are professional ball-players," the *Chronicle* informed its readers. "They give entertainments and charge an admission fee, and the public does not lose sight of the fact that they are as much open to criticism as the performers in a circus, burnt-cork artists, or disciples of the sock and buskin."

History was made again in 1935 when Crosley Field hosted the first night game in the history of Major League Baseball. The Reds played the Phillies and beat them. At the time everyone thought of baseball as an afternoon game, a game played in daylight, but night baseball opened the door for the sport to have a much larger following on television. I miss day games myself. I used to love watching World Series games played during the day, but I guess they feel they won't make enough money on advertising if they put even one game on during the afternoon.

For us, the Reds were the story of baseball. Every season opened with a Reds home game, and that was how it ought to be, too. Back in the 1940s and '50s, sports was all we had. We didn't have iPhones. We didn't have iPads. We didn't have computers. We didn't have huge, high-definition TVs that pulled in hundreds of channels. We just had going outside and playing sports or watching sports.

Back then you used your own imagination, you dreamed your own dreams, you didn't have everything stuffed into your head. You can't even call the little box we had at the house when I was growing up a TV in the same sense that what people watch now is a TV. Now there's super-slow-mo and high definition and the rotation on the ball shows up so clear, you can be half-blind and still see it. The picture was so fuzzy on our little box of a TV that it was more like a glorified radio. You'd hear the crack of the bat against the ball and then try to follow the progress of the tiny little ball on the screen.

Mostly that would make you want to run outside and play your own ball games, and that was what we did, and what all the other kids in the neighborhood did, too. Everyone wanted to be a baseball player, and that meant all the best athletes were playing baseball, even if like me they also loved football. Our Knothole League wasn't any different than Little League, the rules were the same, you played on the same field, it was just organized differently and not sanctioned by the same rules, which was too bad. When I was twelve years old, we had a great team in Cincinnati. If we'd been eligible, I'm sure we'd have gone all the way to the Little League World Series.

From an early age, I always took the attitude that every time you stepped out on a baseball field and played in front of fans, any fans, you'd better give it your all. Going back to when I was nine, ten, eleven years old, I figured if I couldn't come to the ballpark and bust my ass for a couple hours, what was wrong with me? I knew that if I ever *didn't* run a ground ball out, I'd live to regret it. That would be the one the shortstop booted. As soon as I didn't run out a pop-up, some fielder was going to drop it and I'd be standing there in between first and second looking for a hole to climb down into and hide from the world. That was why I played the way I did. I didn't play the game any differently as an adult. I played hard-nosed baseball at Crosley Field and I played hard-nosed baseball back at Boldface Park.

CHAPTER 3

Not the Best Baseball Player

There was one thing my family never did when I was a kid: vacations. No Florida Everglades. No Yellowstone. No Disneyland. No nothing. And I mean never! Our one family tradition was every summer we'd pile into the car and make the seventy-mile drive along River Road to Madison, Indiana, for the annual Madison Regatta. We'd drive back the same day. Everyone in the family loved going to see those big hydroplane boats racing up and down the Ohio River. I remember when I was eleven, Burnett Bartley won the regatta with his boat *Wildcatter*; the next year we came back, and darned if Burnett Bartley and *Wildcatter* didn't win the whole thing again.

My dad wasn't about to take the family on a real vacation for one very simple reason: He'd promised my Knothole League coach, Red Grothaus, he wouldn't. Every year, he would pull aside my coach for a private talk.

"My son will never miss a practice," my dad would tell the coach.

"He'll never miss a game. He'll play all out, all the time. But your pact with me is: *If there is a right-hander pitching, I want him to bat left-handed, and if there's a left-hander pitching, I want him to bat right-handed.*"

My dad had decided when I was nine years old that he wanted me to be a switch batter, and he was going to make sure I got my swings in from both sides of the plate. On the other hand, my coach claims I was the one who approached him. "He came up to me and asked if he could bat left-handed against a right-handed pitcher. I said, 'Sure, but if you don't swing level, you're going to turn around and bat right-handed.'"

I wasn't going to do that. I'd been practicing.

"So he hits a line drive between first and second base for a single," Red remembers.

My dad would never have considered leaving town and having me miss games. In those days that was pretty typical. Families would leave on vacation and all of a sudden the Knothole League team was without its star player. My dad wouldn't do that. My dad didn't even want me to go to the movies, because he thought it was bad for my eyes.

For most big league baseball players, you can go back to when they were coming up and they stood out at every level. I stood out because I played so hard, not because my talent jumped out at people. Still, I had confidence and a sense of purpose that were unusual. I put everything into whatever I was doing. My Knothole teammate John Rewwer remembers it this way: "I'll never forget walking past the stands at a local ballpark one day and overhearing a couple of men say, 'That kid is going to be in the major leagues someday.' Pete never really excelled—he was flashy and everything, but he was no Eddie Brinkman growing up."

I wasn't the best player on my high school team and I wasn't even the best player on my Knothole League team. I had Eddie Brinkman on my teams, and he always stood out. He was close to six feet tall while he was still in high school, and strong, too. He was the Babe Ruth of Cincinnati, just an exceptional young athlete.

Brinkman caught everyone's eye back then. I never did. "He wanted to be a major leaguer in the worst way," Brinkman said later, about me. "That was all he cared about."

As an example, in November 1954, when I was thirteen years old, I hit a home run in the Knothole League tournament to help my team, Hi Hi Mutual Aid, to a 9–0 victory. But Ed Brinkman hit a home run in that game, too! He went on to play for the Washington Senators for many seasons and spent fifteen years in the big leagues.

Eddie and I grew up about a mile apart but went to different schools when we were small, so we only really got to know each other as Knothole teammates when we were nine. He recalls, "I was small myself at the time, but Pete was really tiny, even smaller than me. That was my first year of playing organized baseball of any kind. Pete was the catcher, and I think he caught because he could catch the ball. Besides, I don't think anyone else wanted to put the catcher's gear on. I played mostly outfield—they put me someplace where I couldn't hurt anybody. We didn't have a very good team. We had a bunch of kids from down along the river. They called us 'river rats.' We had just enough kids to field a team, really."

I was always proud of being a river rat, growing up on the west side of Cincinnati. We weren't poor, but we weren't the fancy people. We had to work a little harder for everything in life, and that always suited me just fine.

Red Grothaus would tell people later that I was probably no better than third-best on those Knothole League teams he coached in those years. "By their last year in Class B, Eddie Brinkman was much further ahead than Pete. Eddie used to knock the cover off the ball and he had a much better glove and arm than Pete. His bat went south on him when he got to the major leagues. And we had another kid, Bernie Wrublewski, who's now in the seminary. He was better than both of them. We played everybody, but those three never came out. We alternated between pitcher, catcher, and shortstop. They were 100 percent better than the other kids. I thought Eddie and Bernie were definitely major league prospects. I thought Pete was too small."

People who saw me then couldn't believe all the running I did. I'd have my catcher's gear on in the dugout, and as soon as we made the last out, I sprinted out onto the field. Then when we got the third out and it was our turn up at the plate, I sprinted back to the dugout and grabbed a bat and started swinging. I was always trying harder than anyone else. Which goes back to: Why walk when you can run? Why not run to first even on a base on balls?

"If I had done that, I'd probably have weighed 125 pounds," Brinkman said later. "Pete's always had an amazing amount of energy. He's always had trouble sitting down for even five minutes."

When I was fifteen years old going out for American Legion ball, I was cut from the team. I was five-foot-seven, maybe 135 pounds at the time. I hated getting cut—and my dad might have hated me getting cut even more than I did. He was disappointed, but he knew the issue was never with my heart. I was just too small.

"You've got to learn from this," he told me in a calm, strong voice. "Just keep working hard. You'll get your chance."

I'd always listened to everything he said before then, but afterward, I was even more focused on working hard and giving everything I had to be a better athlete and prove any doubters wrong. I started as a catcher, which is the best way to learn the game. I knew I'd be involved in every play. You're right in the thick of the action behind home plate, and every time the ball is thrown you've got a chance of catching it. If you're playing right field, you might stand out there for two days and never get a fly ball. Catching when I was young helped me understand baseball at a deeper level. It helped keep me alert. It forced me to think along with every pitch and every play. They always say that old catchers make the best managers. Maybe at heart I'm an old catcher, even though that was the only position I never did play in the big leagues—besides pitcher and shortstop.

When I was a kid, it was just like later—you could always spot me by the dirt stains on my uniform. But I always had good equipment, good shoes, a good glove, a good bat, whatever was necessary to make me a better player. My dad always said he wanted me to look good in case I didn't play good.

My team, S&H Green Stamps, won what they called the Knothole League Class A national championship in August 1956, when I was fifteen years old. I had a triple and a single in the championship game and we won 10–0. Brinkman and I had played together on a team that won the Knothole city championship two years earlier, but this was bigger than that.

Football was my best sport, though. I was always the best football player on every team I played on up through high school. Size was an issue again. I was the little pipsqueak who wouldn't go down. You couldn't tackle me. I had those quick hips. They called my dad Old Swivel Hips, and I did my best to be a chip off the old block. My dad would always be telling me who to watch and what to watch for. He told me who was fundamentally sound, who practiced the right way, and who played the right way. He had a great eye for athletes and he was smart about coaches, too.

Seeing sports through my dad's eyes made all the difference for me. I didn't just watch him, I didn't just talk through the games with him, I lived that experience with him. He transferred more to me than knowledge or insight; he passed on something deep and private and urgent, a kind of ornery hunger never to be satisfied with anything but giving your all—and winning.

Starting in 1949, when I was just eight years old, the University of Cincinnati got a new football coach by the name of Sid Gillman. He coached the Bearcats for only five seasons, before he moved on to a job as head coach of the Los Angeles Rams, but for those five years my father would take me to see University of Cincinnati games whenever he could. It seemed he could always manage to get us tickets for the Bearcats. They didn't play Big Ten teams Ohio State or Purdue. They were going up against teams like Loyola and Tulsa, not exactly football powers, but I didn't care. I was just a kid, tagging along with my dad. I couldn't wait to get out of the house and go watch a game, any game.

My dad and I watched so much sports together, from Oscar Robertson to Sid Gillman's exciting University of Cincinnati teams to as many Reds games as we could, that we had an understanding that ran deep. Later, when I was in the big leagues, people would hear stories about how it was with my dad growing up, and they'd get the wrong idea. Yes, it was true, winning was everything to my dad. That was how he approached every game as an athlete, even when he was in his forties, still playing football, still scoring touchdowns, still the toughest sumbitch out there. That was how he saw my games, too, even if I was ten or eleven or twelve years old. Sports to us were a calling. They were a way of life. You were dishonoring the entire idea of sports if your goal was less than total focus on winning.

So, let's say one of my Knothole League teams just had a tough game. Let's say I went 4 for 4 with a triple and a double, but the team lost by one run. On the way home, no food. That was the rule. I only got to eat after a game if my team had won. That might sound harsh, but it made sense to me. My stomach would be grumbling and growling and that would feel right in a way, because I wanted to be unhappy, thinking about losing. I wanted to find a way to do more next time to carry my team. Winning was always in my blood, and having to win to eat sure helped reinforce that. Above all, my dad wanted me to have the pride of a champion.

"Understand that you represent all of us out there, every Rose," my dad would say to me.

My dad was a stickler, but he was always supportive. I knew he believed in me. The dialogue that we had about how I was going to make it was matter-of-fact. He wasn't wishing for anything, he wasn't hoping, he was just spelling out the ins and outs of making it as an athlete.

"Always back up every throw," he would tell me, "because you can be sure the one time you don't hustle over to be in position to back up first base, a throw will be wide and you won't be there and you'll be kicking yourself."

That went for everyone. When the ball is hit, every player on the field should be moving, because if you're not, that white rat will find you. Strange things happen. Everybody has to be backing up a base. A guy might throw to the wrong base. He might overthrow his man. On a baseball field the ball can end up anywhere. The worst thing in the world is if you didn't back up the throw. My dad didn't tolerate mental errors.

He was realistic about his own success. He knew that he had some quality that made him rise to the occasion when it really mattered, whether he was playing football or baseball or boxing, and he had a pretty clear idea he'd passed whatever quality that was on to me. He just wanted me to be realistic about my size and how I was going to have to work harder and be smarter than everyone else if I was going to overcome that.

So, if I went 4 for 6 in a game and on the way home he ignored the four hits and wanted to talk about what I'd done the other two times, I might not have liked it, but I understood. My dad and I were so close, it was almost like talking to myself. He'd talk to me about a 2–0 pitch down in the zone that I could have stayed down on and stroked right back up the middle for a clean base hit, but instead I'd swung from my ass. I'd let myself get caught up with visions of the long ball dancing in my head, trying to hit a big home run to impress my teammates and maybe a few girls, but that was not my game. I was too small to be a Babe Ruth type.

My dad was always going over every game of mine he saw. Why didn't I back up on that play? Did I notice when a player on the other team looked to be injured and was probably going to be slower? Was I always mentally ready to go back out on defense, with my catcher's gear on as soon as I came back to the dugout after an at bat? Everything you could think about on the field my dad had thought about, and it was a master class in the subtle art of winning baseball games. This wasn't *Baseball for Dummies.* This was *Baseball for Winners.*

CHAPTER 4

Passed Over

I had a great year of football as a high school freshman. I was too small at that point for anyone to think I had much of a future in football, at least until I hit a major growth spurt, but I could run the ball and I could score touchdowns. I was known more as a football player than a baseball player back then. "He just had a real talent for changing directions at full speed," Thomas Moore, another running back at my high school, said later.

Red Grothaus, who had coached me in baseball for six seasons, also coached me on two straight undefeated Pee Wee city championship football teams. He understood better than any coach back then that whatever the sport, I was going to find a way.

"The ability that Pete had was nothing compared to Ted Williams," Red said later. "He just worked harder at it. Pete's a totally self-made man, a testament to hard work. He was totally wrapped up in whatever he was doing. If it was baseball, he'd work like the devil. If it was football, the same way. Basketball . . . boxing . . . horseshoes . . . anything."

He got that right. I loved playing football. Even more than baseball, football was going into battle, and I loved going into battle. That was how I saw everything, as a battle I was going to win, come what may.

"I remember our quarterback got racked up by the other team," Joe Scherer, my teammate on the Price Hill Kiwanis Pee Wee football team said later. "They were taking him away in an ambulance. Pete gathered everybody around and raised all kinds of hell about it. He was saying, 'They knocked out our quarterback. We have to get them back.' He was very adamant about it."

Hell yes, I was adamant. I always liked to talk. I was known as a chatterbox on the field and in the dugout, and later on, anytime a sportswriter came to me looking for a quote, I did my best to oblige. But the real language of sports has nothing to do with words. You define yourself—as a player, as a team—through what you do when the game is on the line. You might lose a game, but in the bigger picture you lose only if you don't give your all. When I say give your all, I'm not just talking about running hard, playing with a lot of energy, all that stuff. I'm also talking about being smart and being honest and noticing everything. When the other team knocks your quarterback out of the game, you either rise up and meet that challenge or they walk off winners. That was never something I was going to let happen on any of my teams, and you bet, if I was on it, it was my team, that was the way I saw it. Even if I wasn't the biggest guy, or the best athlete, I was always the biggest competitor, and sooner or later everyone knew that.

I'd been a star of the freshman team, but a year later I'd be a sophomore, trying to make the varsity team. That would mean playing against bigger, older guys, but that didn't faze me in the least. Bring 'em on! That was my attitude.

I never had that chance. There was no open tryout for varsity football. They had to invite you—and they didn't invite me. My backup at running back, Charlie Schott, got invited, because he was bigger than me and probably faster, too. I was left out in the cold, and believe me, it was damn cold out there, colder than a witch's tit.

Everyone hates losing, but I hated it more. That's how I was brung up. My dad was a legend of Cincinnati sports, and no son of Big Pete was ever going to be left off a team. Only that was just what happened. Usually I shrugged it off when something didn't go my way. As a ballplayer, if you can't shrug it off, you've got no future. You'll never hit again if you're carrying around the baggage of all those times you missed a ball you should have creamed or came up short in one of a hundred different ways. That's all water under the bridge.

Missing out on playing football when I was a sophomore in high school was nothing I could shrug off. It hit me like a ton of bricks. I read somewhere that a shark can't even breathe right if it isn't moving forward on the attack. Is that right? Well, that was me. I couldn't breathe if I couldn't play. I couldn't breathe if I couldn't compete. I needed in the worst way to be out there on our sandlot practice field or across the street at Trechter Stadium, scoring a touchdown or throwing a block or kicking a field goal. I needed to be in the thick of the action. That was where I felt like myself. That was where I was grinding out my future somehow.

Nothing about being left off the varsity team as a sophomore made sense to me. Sure I was small, but I always gave more to a game than anyone else out there, and I found the end zone. Why couldn't they see that I could help the team?

And how could I live without football? How could I talk sports with my dad if I wasn't even able to play football as a sophomore? My dad always said I was representing the whole Rose family every time I went out there. So the whole Rose family had been rejected? Denied? Dishonored? It was a bigger load than I could carry at that age. I felt so bad about disappointing my father, not living up to his example, that I felt like I couldn't do anything.

So I stopped going to school. I just said: "Fuck school! I ain't going!" I'd leave home like I was going to go to school, but I wouldn't go to school. If I couldn't play football, how was I going to sit still in one of those classes and try to pretend to half listen for a while? It just wasn't going to happen. I found a lot of ways to spend my time that didn't involve going to school. I'd go swim across the Ohio River with a friend or two. I'd go down to Boldface Park and look for some kids who wanted to play pickup ball. Or I'd ride my bike down to Schulte's Fish Garden near the Anderson Ferry landing and throw the ball against the wall. I might have had a reputation for being a wild kid, but I wasn't really all that wild.

"Pete had his scrapes, but he was not a kid who got in that much trouble," my high school's quarterback, Ralph Griesser, remembers. "Maybe he appeared to others as a dead-end kid, because that was his look, but I don't think anyone considered him a problem, other than academically. He had a few borderline friends from the neighborhood, but he also had friends who were solid people. One of his friends became a high school principal and another became a priest. How bad were those guys?"

I always liked talking to all kinds of different people. That was just the way I was. Maybe it was like my dad when he would work down at the bank as a teller: If you couldn't talk to all different kinds of people, you were at a disadvantage. I didn't think I was better than anyone and I sure as hell didn't think anyone was better than me, either.

I was never book smart. I was never one for reading. I didn't mind skipping out on school and not having to do those lessons, but it wasn't about being a bad student, it was about not being able to play football. That was why I flunked my sophomore year. I'd always worked in class so that I could stay eligible for sports. And now that motivation was gone.

The next year, I was back playing football. I'd grown some, and I made the varsity team my second sophomore year. I wasn't a star of the team at that point, but at least I was playing again. By the next year I was all-city as a junior. As one newspaper put it that October, "Western's grid machinery revolves around Quarterback Ralph Griesser, Pete Rose, and Charlie Schott." On November 15, 1958, we beat Walnut Hills 21–12 and I scored a touchdown on a fifty-seven-yard run.

Griesser went on to play quarterback at Michigan. "Pete was very small, but quick," he said later. "He would do things like you would see on the cartoons—disappear into the pile and come out on the other side. Even on film, you couldn't see how he did it. He was very competitive, very tough, and had great hands. I would throw him little dump passes and away he would go, without blocking. He put on a show."

Being smaller had its advantages. My legs were strong and I had good balance and good anticipation. That was part of it. Determination took over from there. If I got the ball, I wasn't going down without a good fight. One time against Central High School, they caught it on film when I went for a long run.

"Pete went something like thirty-five yards for a touchdown," my teammate Jim Wietholter remembered, "which doesn't sound like a particularly great accomplishment, except that he had lost his helmet, had his jersey torn, and had at least two guys holding on to him as he went over the goal line. And if you look closely at the whole play, you can see that all eleven players on defense touched him at one time or another during that run."

Our archrival was Elder High School, and later in November we routed them 31–14, even better than our 29–13 win over them back in 1932. I made a one-handed catch to score one of our touchdowns.

Our school yearbook had a picture of me on the football field, surrounded by guys trying to tackle me while I stayed on my feet. The caption reads: "Pete Rose, West Hi's shifty scatback, twists and turns his way through three Hughes defenders on his way to a score."

Still, my size was a big strike against me. As Griesser later explained it, "College recruiters came to see us, and they rated six or seven others ahead of Pete. His biggest qualities were not overpowering skills, but he didn't back away from any man or anything."

Back away? I don't even know the meaning of the words. Back away? I never once in my entire life backed away, not from a fight, not from a challenge. That's just not how I was raised. My dad shaped me in so many ways, but I guess I picked up some of my fire from my mother as well. She was tough, my mom.

"I didn't take nothing from nobody," she said later in life. "I wouldn't stand back from a fight. A couple of times I pulled a girl out of a bar and whupped the hell out of her. One time, I was already married, I was in my mid-twenties, and I already had a couple of kids. She was telling somebody I was running around with her husband. I went right in the Trolley Tavern and I dragged her out, and I knocked the living hell out of her. We were real, real good friends. I don't know why she ever started something like that, but I just went in and grabbed her."

I'd been cut from my American Legion baseball team when I was younger, but by the time I was seventeen I was starring on the team. We had one game in July 1958 where we won 25–0 in an Ohio-Kentucky American Legion game and the other team didn't even get a hit. The newspaper for that game said: "Pete Rose led Postal Employees' parade of home runs by slamming out two."

Then again, if you read my high school yearbook describing the season for our baseball team my junior year, I barely get a mention. "Sophomore Eddie Brinkman proved his worth as an outstanding pitcher, a slick fielding third baseman, and a fine hitter," the text read. "Eddie is a fine prospect for the future. Maury Bibent, another Soph., caught well all year and Walt Harmon and Pete Rose, Junior, both earned starting positions."

My high school coach was Paul Nohr, but we all called him Pappy, because he was like everybody's dad. Pappy was short and fat, so it wasn't like he was out there taking ground balls and showing you how to turn a double play, but none of my coaches did that. We just kind of practiced it and knew how to practice. They knew how to tell us how to do it, but they didn't show us how to do it.

Pappy Nohr had started coaching at Western Hills when it opened in 1928, and he was a great coach. Nine of his players went on to play in the big leagues, which is amazing enough—Chuck Brinkman, Eddie Brinkman, Dick Drott, Art Mahaffey, Russ Nixon, Clyde Vollmer, Herm Wehmeier, Don Zimmer, and me. You know what's even more amazing? Four of his players went on to become major league managers as well. Don Zimmer, of course, as well as Russ Nixon, Jim Frey, and me.

Pappy was the one who turned me into a second baseman. "He wanted to play catcher," he said later. "We had a good catcher, so we put him at second base. . . . Young Pete was a hard worker, but he never did win honors for high school baseball—good bunter, ran hard, ran out everything, but he wasn't the fastest guy on the team. Attitude, that's what they talk about now, isn't it? The kid had a great attitude."

No one was thinking of me then as a future big league baseball player. Playing for my high school team in 1959, I was chosen for the *Post* and *Times-Star*'s annual Hamilton County high school all-star team as a second baseman, but I was named to the second team, not the first team.

The next year, just as I was starting to fill out and grow a little, I was out of eligibility. Because I'd flunked and had to repeat my sophomore year, by the time I was a senior I couldn't play baseball for Western Hills anymore—and I couldn't play football, either. It's funny to think about now. If I could have played one more year, and picked up where I left off as a running back, I probably would have ended up going to college somewhere to play football and not pursued baseball, at least not at that time. Even without playing my senior year, I almost went to the University of Tennessee in Knoxville on a football scholarship. I went down there on a visit. They were interested in me, but going to college made no sense to me. That would have been more school, the last thing I wanted.

CHAPTER 5

Uncle Buddy

I don't know what I would have done if not for my uncle Buddy. He was my ace in the hole. I don't know what would have become of me if I hadn't gone through high school knowing that because of Uncle Buddy, I always had a shot at achieving my dream of one day playing for the Cincinnati Reds, no matter how unlikely that might have seemed to everyone else but me.

Getting passed over for the varsity football team when I was a sophomore ate me up, and it ate me up seeing other guys have growth spurts so that they were a lot bigger and stronger than me. I could always play, but I was too damn small to catch any scout's eye—any scout but Buddy Bloebaum, my mom's brother, who in those days worked as what they called a bird-dog scout for the Cincinnati Reds. I can tell you for sure that if I hadn't had Uncle Buddy, I'd have never had a chance to play professional baseball.

Buddy might have been the best baseball player in our family. He was big and strong, six-foot-two, 190 pounds, and played shortstop. He was born in 1903, and just when he was getting his shot in baseball, the Great Depression hit. In 1932, when he was twenty-nine, Buddy played one season with the Cedar Rapids Bunnies, the Reds' D-League affiliate in the Mississippi Valley League, and batted .281 with twenty-three doubles and seven triples. It was news in Richmond, Indiana, when the local baseball team, the Lincos, signed Buddy in October 1934. A couple days later, the *Palladium-Item* in Richmond wrote that local fans "fell in love with" my uncle Buddy.

"He runs bases 'à la Tyrus Raymond Cobb style' and he hits hard and often," the paper wrote. "He singled and doubled, scored twice, was hit by a pitched ball. . . . His double was hardly more than an ordinary single, hit hard into right field, but he rounded first and went speeding on towards second." That forced an error and Buddy went all the way to third, then scored on an infield single. That was the way Buddy played, always doing everything he could to beat you.

Buddy could also hit from both sides of the plate. That was why my dad decided to turn me into a switch batter at nine years old, because he saw what Buddy accomplished. Buddy told my dad, "If Pete has an opportunity to be a switch batter, it's a big asset."

Buddy was also a great pool player and made some money with his cue stick. He was a pool shark, one of the best around. He had great eyes and could shoot pool equally well right-handed or left-handed. He used to get his name in the paper for winning tournaments.

But Buddy was too sharp a pool player for his own good—no one wanted to play him anymore. He couldn't make any money. So he took to wearing a black mask and taking on challengers as the Masked Marvel, or he would just put on an exhibition of trick shots. I remember he had a nice pool table in his basement and tried to teach me how to shoot pool, but I didn't have the patience. I was just in awe watching him.

My parents bought me a great graduation present: a car. That was a big deal. Our family didn't even own a car all the time when I was a kid. We didn't have much money, and my dad took the bus to work, so why would we need one? My dad bought me a dark blue 1937 Plymouth for a hundred bucks. It had no bumper on the front, but I loved that Plymouth. As far as I was concerned, the best thing about that car was it had a stereo right in the middle, which I always had cranked up. I'd listen to anything, but mostly it was Chuck Berry and those kinds of guys. Later I traded that '37 Plymouth in for a '51 Chevy that had a California rake so it tilted back.

Since I couldn't play high school baseball my senior year, I had to find some other way to keep developing. Uncle Buddy lived in Dayton, about an hour's drive north of Cincinnati. He worked at the National Cash Register Company south of Dayton. Uncle Buddy said I could play in something called the Dayton Double-A amateur league. I'd be playing for a new team, Lebanon, managed by Chuck Shoop, a local teacher and coach. Most of the games were played in Dayton, an easy enough drive in my '37 Plymouth. It wasn't a chickenshit league. It was definitely a step up from high school and great for my development. It was amateur, but each team could have three players with minor league experience, what they called class players.

Lebanon's three class players were two left-handed pitchers, Jack Wantz and Jerry Leak, and shortstop Don Pierce, but maybe their best player was Sonny Webb, our center fielder. I ended up hanging around a lot with Sonny and another black guy on that team who was a top-notch player, George Thatcher, our third baseman, who had played for the Cincinnati Tigers in the Negro Leagues and might have ended up with the Reds if his eye had not been badly hurt in a freak accident when a teammate hit him with a ball.

Sonny had grown up in the Walnut Hills section of Cincinnati, idolizing the Negro Leagues player Lou Dula, who lived in the neighborhood and would come over to his house to play cards with his parents and tell stories about playing for the Homestead Grays. Sometimes Dula would even play stickball out front with Sonny and the other neighborhood kids.

Sonny was invited to the Reds' 1958 spring training in Laredo, Texas, and played well but did not make the team. He ended up playing for the Detroit Stars of the Negro Leagues but still hoped to land a spot with the Reds when he and I were playing together for the Lebanon team.

We used to play every Wednesday and Sunday. I got off to a bit of a slow start, but a couple weeks into the season I was on a roll. The *Dayton Daily News* headline on May 18, 1960, was ROSE BATS KIDDIE CORPS PAST BAILEY.

"Rose, Western Hills high school senior, had five hits in five times at bat," the article read. "The Cincinnati youth, who was a standout in two sports, football and baseball, may attend either Miami or the University of Cincinnati or may be lured into professional ball by the Cincinnati Reds."

I was hitting the shit out of the ball while facing pretty good pitchers, much better pitchers than I would have had in high school. By the first week of June I was third in the league with a .483 average, which was a lot better than I'd ever hit in high school. On June 12

I had two triples, a double, and a single to carry us to an 8–2 win over Dorothy Lane Market, the defending champions, and move us one game out of first place.

Since my uncle Buddy lived in Dayton, he came to a lot of the games, and he was able to pass on reports to the Reds of how I was doing. I was so small at the time, it was going to take some convincing to get the Reds interested, but at least I was giving Buddy plenty to tell them about. Tommy Thompson, another scout for the Reds, was also in my corner and kept urging them to take me seriously. Carl Ackerman, a full-time Reds scout who was Buddy's boss, was also talking me up, but my size was working against me.

"The trouble was," Ackerman remembered later, "he was such a skinny little runt in those days. He was like five seven and a half and maybe 150 pounds, if you weighed him soaking wet."

That's where my ace in the hole came in: Uncle Buddy had watched my dad develop. He knew that when my dad was twenty-one, he was special weight boxing champion of Ohio, fighting at 112 pounds. But he grew into a 190-pound football player! The men in my family matured late physically, and Buddy kept telling Ackerman and the Reds that that was going to be true for me—and it was. I was 155 pounds when I got out of high school and two and a half years later I was in the big leagues at 202 pounds.

The way I was hitting the ball in the Dayton Double-A League, other teams were bound to show interest as well. Jack Baker, a bird-dog scout for the Baltimore Orioles, saw me go 5 for 5 and let my dad know his club was interested in me. He convinced his supervisor, Hal Newhouser, to come take a look at me. He flew out to see me just as the Reds were finally showing real interest.

The *Dayton Daily News* ran a picture of me on June 19, 1960, with the caption "Hit-Happy Batter" and an article that explained "Lebanon's Pete Rose is only nineteen, but he's on more than equal footing in the men's world of Class AA amateur baseball. He was leading the league at .500 going into Thursday's Wright-Patterson game. Rose filled in at catcher until replacements arrived, but was back at his normal shortstop position against Dorothy Lane Market last week. Rose tripled twice, doubled, and singled for a perfect day and three runs batted in against the Marketmen in an 8–2 victory to earn The Daily News-Big Guys Amateur Baseball Hall of Fame honors."

That five-hit game when everyone was watching, including some scouts, was just the lift I needed. My only regret was that my dad couldn't be there. That was a long drive up to Howell Field in Dayton, and he couldn't leave work early. All I could think about was telling him about the game.

"When you get home tonight, and your dad asks how many hits you got, just go like this," Uncle Buddy told me, and held his hand up to his face, sliding all five fingers down and grinning.

That's what I did when I got home. I always had to report to my dad, first thing, and that was one time I'll never forget. Uncle Buddy, Tommy Thompson, and Carl Ackerman convinced the Reds to give me a tryout at Crosley Field. I don't remember much about that except how nervous I was. I guess I showed them I could play. Phil Seghi, the Reds' farm director, told Uncle Buddy they were ready to sign me. I got a $7,000 bonus and another $5,000 bonus, contingent on me making the majors. They knew how competitive I was, and understanding that, they gave me things to accomplish to motivate me. And in fairness, when I made the majors less than three years later, they paid up.

Soon the Associated Press was reporting: "The Cincinnati Reds signed another high-school star—Pete Rose of Cincinnati—to a bonus contract. Rose, a 19-year-old second baseman, played with Cincinnati Western Hills High School. He was signed to a contract with the Reds' Nashville farm club in the Southern Association and is to be assigned to Geneva of the New York–Pennsylvania League."

I was sky high. Growing up, all I ever wanted to do was play for the Reds. It was the same for every kid in Cincinnati, just like every kid in Brooklyn wanted to play for the Dodgers. Back in the 1940s and '50s, there were great football players and basketball players, but baseball was at the forefront with the great Dodgers team and the great Yankees team and their larger-than-life players, Babe Ruth and Mickey Mantle and Jackie Robinson and Roy Campanella.

I had a choice. I could do the sensible thing and wait for the next spring, when I could go to the Reds' spring training in Tampa, Florida, with all the other guys, and be on equal footing going into a season for Class D Geneva in the New York–Penn League. That was what the Reds thought I ought to do.

"You're going to have to face facts," Phil Seghi told me. "You're really not in shape to play."

He had a point. I'd hit the ball great in the Dayton Double-A League, but it wasn't like we got together and practiced every day or anything like that. A couple games a week was not enough to have you in real baseball shape and I knew that better than anyone, but I didn't care. I wanted to play ball. I wanted to get started as soon as I could. I wanted to show them—and show myself—that I had what it took to be a big leaguer.

I graduated from high school on Friday, June 17, 1960, signed with the Reds on Saturday, and left on Sunday to fly to Rochester, New York, where I'd take a Greyhound bus to Geneva, New York. I was traveling by airplane for the first time. I climbed up inside and couldn't believe I was up there in that thing. I'd never seen anything like that. I remember after we'd lifted off and were flying along for a while, I finally turned to look out the window. I'll never forget it. The whole time I was asking myself: *What the heck is keeping this airplane in the air?*

PART 2

BUSH LEAGUES

CHAPTER 6

Geneva (Not Switzerland)

I arrived in the town of Geneva (population: 18,000) to play for the Redlegs with two months left in the 1960 New York–Pennsylvania League season and had a lot of catching up to do. For the first time in my life, I was a long ways from home, in a town in upstate New York on the edge of Seneca Lake, one of the Finger Lakes.

Deep down I was just a scared river rat, not knowing what was in front of me, but I've always loved the action so much, the swings, the hits, the backhand stab, the headfirst slide into third, I couldn't wait to play baseball. I was fired up. I guess some might even call that overly enthusiastic.

I arrived at the ballpark in Geneva carrying my suitcase with three bats attached to it. Of course you had to bring your own bats.

"I'm looking for Lefty Venuti," I told someone.

"You've found him," said Lefty. He was the general manager.

"Phil Seghi sent me to play second base for you guys," I said.

"OK, hot dog," Lefty said. "Sit down here and we'll sign this contract."

I went 2 for 5 in my first game. They thought I was brash, but if you're going to be brash, you better hit the ball.

The local press gave me a fair reception, I couldn't complain, talking about how I was aggressive and eager. But what they were thinking was: Who is this guy? Norm Jallow, a reporter for the *Geneva Times*, later told another reporter: "I think a lot of people didn't understand—and I admit, I was one of them—why this clown was running to first on a walk."

I didn't know my teammates in Geneva at first and they didn't know me. That's how it was at that level of the minor leagues, young guys thrown together, just getting their start, and no one knows anyone else. The difference with me was that I had signed late and joined the team late, and most of my teammates had at least gone through spring training together. On a better team I might have found myself getting more of a cold shoulder, but this was not a good team. That Geneva club would finish last in the New York–Penn League that season with a 54–75 record, twenty-nine games behind the first-place Erie Sailors. We weren't a very good team, but we tried hard. We were just happy to be in professional baseball. The Redlegs had the worst pitching in the league and were second-worst in batting. It was all new to me, so I was just trying to get adjusted and learn, but when you join a losing team, it's always more of a challenge.

One of the first things that jumped out at me about that Geneva team was that they already had a second baseman. His name was Tony Perez, and he'd just come from Cuba a couple months earlier. The team decided to move Tony over to third to make room for me at second, and Tony couldn't have handled it better. As he says now, "I was really skinny back then and moved really well on the field, so I had no problem moving to third base so Pete could play second base."

He was the nicest guy in the world, and the first thing I noticed about him, even then at seventeen years old, was that he could hit. At that age you're all just trying to get better, trying to climb the ladder up to the big leagues, and you have enough to think about taking care of your own business, but you noticed talent and I knew Tony and I both had futures in baseball. Tony was it. I loved that guy. We took to calling him Big Dog, or Doggie, and I still call him that to this day. It was a name I gave him because never in my life had I seen anyone who was a better hitter with men on base. He was a dog who wanted to hunt.

He was going through some culture shock and had a major adjustment coming from another country, but he had the best attitude. "The town treated me phenomenally," he says now. "Those two years I spent in Geneva I have nothing bad to say. I never had any problems with the people. My biggest problem was during the games because everything was in English. I had to learn to play the game in another language."

Tony didn't speak much English and it never mattered at all to me. Doggie and I understood each other. The Reds' Triple-A team was still in Havana, the Havana Sugar Kings, so a lot of Cubans were very aware of the Reds. In fact, when Tony was signed by the Reds earlier that year after making a name for himself playing for a team in Camagüey owned by a sugar factory, he was assigned to the Sugar Kings' instructional team in Havana. His bonus was a plane ticket to Miami!

Another teammate in Geneva was Art Shamsky, who was born to Jewish parents who had fled Europe, his father's family coming from Ukraine, his mother's family from Poland. Art and I got along from the start. We were both multi-sport athletes growing up, but he was a good student at University City High School in St. Louis and graduated at age sixteen. He played one season for the University of Missouri before signing with Cincinnati. Art and I both rented rooms for ten bucks a week at Mr. McGuire's rooming house right down the street, along with Jack Erwin and Larry Dovel.

"We hit it off right away," Shammy says now. "We both loved the game of baseball. We were so young, and had a chance to be away from home. Life to us at that point was beautiful. We were making about four hundred dollars a month, but we didn't care. Pete, Tony Perez, and I became very, very good friends. If you would have looked at us then, you'd never have expected that the three of us would go on to the big leagues. We all weighed about 150 pounds apiece. We loved the game. We were not prospects in 1960, to say the least. We were more like suspects."

I'm the first to say I had a lot of work to do at that point. I knew I had a future in the game, but I was only going to earn it by working my butt off every single day, every single play.

"If you had seen Pete then, you would have never believed that he would go on to the big leagues," Art says. "The only thing he did well back then was run hard to first base, whether on a hit or a walk. He wasn't a good hitter. His swing was a little bit choppy. He wasn't a great fielder. And he didn't have a particularly good arm."

Tony and Shammy and Martin Dihigo Jr., son of the great Cuban player and Negro Leagues legend, and the rest of my teammates in

Geneva had an advantage on me in that they'd been to spring training in Tampa at the start of the season and opened the season with Geneva at the start of May. They were a lot further along than I was when I arrived in mid-June, but I never let a difficult situation slow me down. I had to play the game my way.

"I remember so many people calling him a hot dog," Tony Perez says now. "I never thought that way. He was always respected by me, and even players on other clubs. He found a way to win games. Some of the cities we played in, though, the fans would get all over him because of the way he played. He never cared."

No one ran to first like I did. No one was sliding headfirst like I did. If you played the way I played, you showed up a lot of players. You made them look bad. I appreciated it when other players patted me on the back for how hard I played the game, but what I was really thinking was: Everybody should play that way. I played the way the old-timers played: the right way.

I was there to play baseball and nothing else. I didn't worry about things I didn't need to worry about. I had enough of a challenge just making sure I got better every day.

"My first impression of Pete was that he was a hard-nosed, tough-as-nails kind of player who was going to do anything to help the team win," Art Shamsky says now. "His trademark was running as hard as he could to first base. It kind of made you forget about some of his deficiencies. Opposing players didn't like it. They saw it as some sort of hot-dog show, but when you met Pete, you knew he was just a hard-nosed player."

We were young and away from home for the first time in our lives, but I didn't waste much time wondering if I was homesick or not. I did look forward to getting letters from my dad. He'd send one every week, and every one of those letters ended the same way. Right at the end, he'd write, "Love Dad. Keep hustling and win!" To this day that's what I write on balls I sign for people, "Keep hustling and win."

The minor leagues in those days were an education. You were all thrown together to see who would sink and who would swim, and no one was pampered. You had to earn everything you got. That was a rough situation in Geneva when I arrived. There were actually rumors that the team's financial troubles might lead to closing the doors to Shuron Park.

"We are doing all we can to make certain that Geneva continues to operate," the Reds' minor league director Phil Seghi told the *Rochester Democrat and Chronicle* at the end of June. "We have given the community-owned team sufficient money for it to operate until the close of the season, we hope."

They hoped. We'd lost five games in a row in late June and then finally edged Erie 7–6 to end the skid. Seghi mentioned me and a few other players they'd added midseason to try to make the club more competitive and urged fans to hang with us.

"Kids can sense when the town is behind them," he said. "They always give that extra something when they know the local population is with them."

They weren't with me at that point. I still had to earn their support. I did that by playing as hard as I could every day. I had a competitive fire about me and I think some of it rubbed off on other guys. At the end of July, we were at home for a doubleheader with the Wellsville Braves and won both games. They'd plunked Tony Perez in the ribs at one point and I wasn't happy about it.

"A rhubarb occurred in the seventh when second baseman Pete Rose was out at second on a force," the Rochester paper reported. "Rose and Lou Haas exchanged words and then swapped punches while players from both dugouts streamed onto the field. Cooler heads prevailed."

I'd slid hard and knocked Lou Haas on his ass, but it was a clean slide. I was pissed off that their pitcher had hit Tony, who was a quiet guy and never said anything to anyone. I was just getting his back. I couldn't charge the mound when he hit Tony. All I could do was go in hard to second. You could say that wasn't fair: What had the second baseman done? But that was baseball.

We were all just trying to get better. Our manager was an Italian American named Reno de Benedetti, who was born in San Francisco and played nine years in the minors, mostly as an infielder. He had the biggest nose in the world; that was the first thing about him you noticed. He was managing us in Geneva because he had a reputation for being good at working with young, up-and-coming players, and for me that was the first time I was really getting instruction.

I was still learning second base that year. Up until my sophomore year of high school I was always a catcher. You don't get many ground balls catching. So in Geneva those two months, I was working with the coaches on learning my position backward and forward. I never did become a Bill Mazeroski–type second baseman, but I learned the position well enough to earn the right to be in a lineup. I was the first one at the ballpark every day, and I'd take extra work, fielding grounders, working on the double play, practicing my footwork. I had to slap myself in the face all the time. I kept thinking: I hope I don't wake up from this dream.

Reno de Benedetti kept telling me not to let the ball play me. If you lay back on a ball and get it in between hops, that's when it's playing you. You have to follow the ball off the bat and make a quick decision on whether to charge or hold your ground. I've always said that talent is one thing and hard work another, and you don't get to be a great baseball infielder without work any more than you get to be a great concert violinist or mechanic without a lot of work and a lot of repetition. The fields we played on in that league were not exactly smooth like one of the billiard tables where Uncle Buddy made so much money as the Masked Marvel. Bad hops were a daily occurrence. You just had to hang in there and put your mistakes behind you and keep learning, keep doing it the right way, and teach yourself to get better and better.

Now in my case, I had a lot of mistakes to learn from! I had thirty-six errors in seventy-two games. That's a lot, one error for every two games, and the fans would get on me sometimes, especially when I first arrived in Geneva. But to give you an idea, our shortstop, Bruce Montgomery, had thirty-eight errors in about the same number of games.

"Pete arrived and struggled," Tony Perez remembers. "He wasn't a great fielder, but Pete played the position the way he played his entire career, giving everything he had every moment he was on the field. He battled every second he was on the field."

On August 19, Reno de Benedetti was in his office when he got a call from Phil Seghi, the Reds' farm director, asking him to resign. He said no, so they fired him and replaced him with Jack Cassini, a Reds scout. Reno couldn't hide his frustration.

"We just don't have a ball club that can be molded," he told reporters that day. "There is not much talent."

So in a short season of transition for me, I had one more transition, making the adjustment to a new skipper. I was just trying to make a good impression. I had some growing pains as a young ballplayer, and I was scuffling for a while. I remember at one point when I was in a slump, Reds scout Slugger Blomski wrote me a letter to cheer me up.

"Dear Pete," he wrote on Cincinnati Baseball Club letterhead. "Old Blomski hasn't forgotten about you. I have been waiting until you got your feet on the ground. I talked to your Dad after he got back from Erie. He said that you were a little down in the dumps. Breaking into Pro Ball is not a bed of roses. You have to take the bitter with the sweet. Don't get the idea that the manager is down on you. He has a job to do.

"Don't expect a pat on the back in Pro Ball when you have a good night," he continued. "It is your job. You are getting paid to do a job. If he keeps you on third, do the best job that you can. Play any place they ask and keep in the lineup. . . . By all means keep hustling. Don't let a hitting slump interfere with your fielding, just keep taking a level swing and you will get your share of hits."

That letter stayed with me. I never forgot it. I wasn't happy about playing third, even just for a game here or there, because I thought I was better at second base and wanted to put my best foot forward. I realized that was the wrong way to think of it. I realized I was better than that. Just like the way from the age of nine I started hitting from both sides of the plate, since a switch batter helps the team more, I could be flexible and open-minded no matter where they put me. If they wanted me to catch, even at my size, I'd catch!

The other big thing I took from that letter was the idea of never letting a hitting slump get in the way of your fielding. Guys do that all the time. In fact, I'd pay attention when an outfielder on the other team was struggling at the plate, because a lot of times they'd still be replaying their at bats in the outfield, and that was a good time to take an extra base on them. It took a perfect throw to get me, and it's hard to make a perfect throw when you're distracted.

Baseball as I played it on my way up to the big leagues was a lot like life: You make your own luck. You make your own skill by working harder and trying harder than anyone. You run your ass off to first base, every time, even if you walk, and you stretch a single into a double, a double into a triple—and even a triple into a four-bagger—every chance you get. You're always looking for an edge, always looking for an opportunity, and when you see one you pounce. I wasn't the fastest runner; I came up out of my squat at the plate and ran kind of crab-legged, but low to the ground, like when I was a running back making my cuts at Western Hills High. That meant I had great balance and could start and stop—or get a jump. People wouldn't even notice me and then they'd look up and I was halfway to the next base.

"Pete Rose, Geneva second baseman, continues his amazing speed on the bases," the *Rochester Democrat and Chronicle* wrote on August 23, 1960. "Pete added two stolen bases to his growing larceny record."

I did OK at the plate. I batted .277, which was a big comedown from the way I'd been hitting the ball in Dayton Double-A, but this was professional baseball and I knew I'd make some adjustments and make my mark. Tony Perez and Art Shamsky both had batting averages around mine, .279 for Doggie and .271 for Shammy, but Shammy was hitting for power. He led the team that season with eighteen home runs and eighty-six RBIs.

The fans in Geneva weren't sure what to make of me. They loved my energy. They loved the way I attacked the game. But this was a small town, and I was a river rat from Cincinnati. No one was more into the game than me, and that meant whether I was on the field or in the dugout, I might have something to say. If a pitcher was getting me out, that was when I would yell at him the most. I'd get them so riled up, they'd try harder to get me out—and maybe make a mistake.

"Get that shit over!" I'd yell out to the mound.

Or if he was a cunny-thumber, a guy with nothing on his pitches, just working you up and down, in and out, I might yell, "Go warm up!"

"He was a great holler guy," a fan in Geneva named Charles Hickey later told the *Cincinnati Enquirer*. "He used to do a lot of hollering from the dugout and he used some four-letter words. He used to come out with some pretty good terms, and that's what upset a lot of people."

I made all those errors, but it was never because I gave up on a ball. That infield in Geneva was an adventure. Balls bounced this way and that. I'd come into the locker room to change and I'd have bruises all over my shoulders and chest.

"If you'd use that goddamn leather glove instead of your body, you might not be so black and blue," our general manager, Brooks, would tell me.

"But Mr. Brooks, I throw 'em out, don't I?" I'd say.

Those bruises didn't mean nothing to me. Pain was letting a ball get past you. Pain was losing a game. A bruise wasn't pain. A bruise felt good. It told you that you were giving your all.

I'd heard those fans give it to me at times during the season. You expect that when you boot a ball, and I booted some balls. I loved it and I hated it. I was always good and wound up, but that made me even more good and wound up. So at the end of the year when I was voted the fans' favorite player, even topping as nice a guy and fine a ballplayer as Tony Perez, that really meant something to me. It showed me the fans appreciated how hard I worked and how much of myself I gave every time I took the field.

I always played for the fans. I grew up a blue-collar guy in a blue-collar neighborhood and they could call me a lunch-pail player all they wanted: I was a working man and a world-class athlete. Did I bring a lunch pail to the ballpark? Hell yes. That's what a working man does. I worked at swinging the bat, I worked at my fielding, but most of all I worked at getting the most out of myself every second I was playing baseball. Even the people who didn't much like my style saw that I was thinking the game with the best of them. I always knew what base to throw to, always had a jump as a base runner, because I paid attention to every little detail. I was no Joe College. I wasn't gonna be quoting from any books. But when it came to baseball smart, I had something people could see. Maybe it was just that I was so single-minded. You might beat me on a given day, but I was never going to beat myself.

Jack Ralston, who held numerous front office positions for the Geneva Redlegs, said: "They say when he came to the park he was carrying a lunch bucket because he didn't want to take any time off."

I felt I owed the fans that much, working as hard as I could. I looked at myself as an entertainer. Yeah, I was a baseball player, but I was an entertainer. I'm entertaining these people who are paying good bucks to watch me play. I set a record with eighteen stolen bases, and every one of those stolen bases was entertaining. I guarantee it. That's why the fans of Geneva voted me the most popular player— and they even gave me two Samsonite suitcases, which I used the next year, even though I didn't even need any suitcases. All the stuff I had would fit in one duffel bag.

Back home in Cincinnati in the off-season, I wanted to make a little spending money. So my dad asked around and found me a job at Railway Express, loading and unloading boxcars every night from midnight to 8 A.M. The railroad terminal was right behind Crosley Field. Isn't it ironic? I was three hundred yards from the ballpark that off-season, working up more of a sweat there than I ever would playing baseball.

That was some hard work. I'd put on canvas work gloves and put my back into it, because we were lifting some heavy packages. Unloading was always better than loading, so we always wanted to do that.

I don't think I was ever so sore in my life. I was never used to hard labor. I played sports—that was it. That first week of loading up boxcars, my arms ached. Once you do it for a while, the soreness is gone. It's just your job, your way of life, box after box after box, lifting, lifting, lifting. My mom would pack up food for me and I ate as much as I could. By the end of that off-season, I'd added twenty-five pounds of muscle. I needed it, too.

CHAPTER 7

Tampa

showed up in Tampa for spring training in early 1961 and earned my share of double takes. I'd grown another two inches or so, but more important, I'd filled out. All those cases I'd loaded and unloaded for Railway Express had made a difference. That and the fifty swings I took every night with Uncle Buddy's weighted bat. I was the same high-energy Pete Rose, always running to first base, always thinking one play ahead, but now I was starting to look like a ballplayer. I went from a scrawny kid who couldn't hit, couldn't run, and couldn't field to being a bigger kid who could run and play defense. It was all about confidence. When you're a kid in professional baseball, that's what it's all about. The best thing I did was not wait until 1961, the way the Reds wanted me to do, and went to Geneva as soon as I could. Getting that taste of baseball and being away from home really helped me.

There were newspaper reports that I'd been assigned to the Reds' Triple-A team in the International League, Jersey City, along with Shammy, Doggie, and a couple other guys. This was how the *Rochester*

Democrat and Chronicle summed up what I offered, based on my short season at Geneva: "He brought life to a faltering nine with his peppery talk and speed on the bases."

I had work to do. Up until then, no one was giving me much shot of making it to the big leagues, and I wasn't even sure where I'd end up in the Reds' system that season. On April 17, the *Tampa Tribune* was quoting Phil Seghi as saying, "We won't know the full roster until one minute before the opening," and listing me as one of the "infield candidates" who would get a look to move up the ladder in the farm system. Not that I ever had any doubts myself, but that was the backdrop for my first full season in pro ball. Once we got through spring training and the season got started, I didn't waste much time making a mark. I hit a triple with the bases loaded to break a tie and give us the win on Opening Day, and I just kept hitting triples as the season rolled along.

My manager that season was Johnny Vander Meer, whose name carried instant respect in baseball, then and always. Everyone who played in that era, at whatever level, knew just what he had done, and no matter how many times you heard it, you still had to shake your head in amazement. He'd pitched back-to-back no-hitters in the big leagues, and he'd done it as a rookie. The first came on Knothole Day at Crosley Field in June 1938 when he shut out Casey Stengel's Boston Bees, 3–0. Four days later, pitching for the Reds at Ebbets Field, Vandy pitched another no-hitter! It was amazing. No one has ever matched that feat and I doubt they ever will.

I loved Johnny Vander Meer. He was a low-key kind of manager, someone who did not speak unless he really had something to say, and he was very fair with me. Even then I came across to some people as cocky, and that rubbed some people the wrong way. They said I hadn't done anything in professional baseball to back that up, and they had a point. Two months of D ball in Geneva with a .277 average and an error every second game was not exactly lighting the league on fire.

I was never cocky. My enthusiasm and intensity just came across to some people that way. Was it cocky to run to first on a walk? Or if you were hit by a pitch? I didn't think so. That was just me being me. That was just me wanting to give everything I had to winning and playing the game right. I'd been raised from the time I was a boy to play as hard as I could every time out there; I didn't know any other way to play and couldn't have done it any other way. That's why it never bothered me what other people thought. I figured the more they watched me, the more they'd understand I wasn't doing it for show, I was doing it because it helped teams win.

Johnny kept his eyes and his mind open when it came to me. He would watch and come to his own conclusions. I'd been assigned to the second team—the scrub team, some called it. A Reds scouting report from Geneva had made it sound like I had no shot at all of ever hitting the big leagues. Someone from the team actually showed it to my dad.

"Pete Rose can't make a double play, can't throw, can't hit left-handed, and can't run," the scouting report had said.

My dad was upset by that, but the way I saw it, that was just an opinion. And opinions were made to be changed. Even I had to admit that the odds of me making the big leagues were looking long at that point. But so what? What difference did it make what the odds were? The only thing I cared about was getting a chance to work hard and get better and show what I could do, and I had that chance playing for the Reds' farm team in Tampa. The scouting reports said I couldn't hit left-handed and made it sound like being a switch batter was something I ought to give up. No way, no how. I'd let my bat speak for itself.

I knew I'd get an honest look from my new manager and I made the most of it. John Vander Meer liked what he saw.

"Pete Rose looked to me like one wonderful hitter," he said later, although he also commented, "Hitting and speed are not his greatest assets. It's aggressiveness."

Vander Meer had me leading off from Opening Day and I repaid his trust in me. We were a hot team and I was leading the way. As the *Tampa Tribune* put it that April 26, "Leadoff man Pete Rose continued to come up with timely blows. He, too, had a triple."

The next week the paper was gushing: "The Tampa Tarpons continued to look like the best thing the Florida State League has seen in a long, long time. Leadoff man Pete Rose socked his eighth triple of the year and a single to keep his hitting streak going to eleven games. He is sporting a .426 mark."

That opened some eyes, but what really got people talking was my triples. I had eleven triples by the first week of May, seventeen triples by the first week of June, and on June 19 I picked up my twentieth triple, putting me four back of the Florida State League season record with half a season still left to play.

Vander Meer loved it. "Every time I looked up he was driving one into the alleys and running like a scalded dog and sliding head-first into third. . . . Speed is the thing in this league. The parks are so big, it's foolish to go for a home run."

I was never fast, but I was always a good base runner. I was fast enough, and I paid attention. The key to legging out a triple was to think triple the second you made contact. That was what my dad always taught me and that was what I had on my mind every single time I was up there. Other guys might poke a line drive into the gap and assume it would be a double and run at three-quarters speed. I didn't do anything three-quarters. I ran all out, digging for first and taking my turn like a man with a train to catch. You had to know when to challenge an outfielder and when not to and I loved trying to guess right on that one.

People think it's as simple as knowing which outfielders have a good arm and which don't, but there's much more to it than that. Let's say you know the center fielder on the other team is in a slump, and he just struck out in the first inning. If you've hit a ball to right-center, you know he's thinking about that strikeout and the O-fer game the day before and is likely to be distracted. If it takes a perfect throw to get you, running all out and diving into third base, then you like your odds running on a guy you know is distracted.

One of my teammates that year was another player from Western Hills High in Cincinnati, Ronnie Flender, an outfielder who signed with the Reds the year before I did. He hit .283 and walked a lot and played a few years in the minors, but never made it past Double-A. Still, for me, it was good having someone around who had also played for Pappy Nohr and with all those other good ballplayers who came out of that program. My teammates also included two pitchers I knew from the season before in Geneva, Larry Dovel, a big right-hander, and Jack Erwin, a lefty. Neither of them ever made the big leagues. We were all so broke, making just four hundred bucks a month, and none of us had a car. We had a lot of fun together, though.

This was all part of growing up. Players don't go through that today, and I think we were better off for having to pay some real dues in Class D ball. To us, playing in the pros was an honor. I can't speak for today's players, but I know that for me and the players I was with that year in Tampa, we knew it was difficult to make the Major Leagues. There were eight teams in the National League and eight teams in the American League then, sixteen teams total compared to the thirty you have now. There were limited spots in the big leagues and it was competitive. It was a big deal to make the big leagues back in them days.

I had so many different nicknames, I couldn't keep track. One was Scooter Rose. Another was Hollywood Rose. I had to go through that shit in the minor leagues because guys would see me do the things I did and say, "Screw him, he's a hot dog," but then they'd see me do it for a week, a month, a year, and they'd know it was legitimate. That's just who I was as a ballplayer. I had to be myself and I couldn't play any other way. So I never really gave a shit if people thought I was some kind of hot dog. I was laughing at them, because all I was trying to do was beat their asses, every time, and if they were losing time wondering if I was a hot dog, then I'd already won. They weren't going to beat me. I knew that.

I'd never really thought about it before, but it hit me recently that my style of play helped free my teammates to go all out. Guys didn't want to be known as "Hollywood" or a showboat. You didn't want your peers to think you were a hot dog. I think I made it easier for other players on my team to come out of their shells. I set an example and it was like, *It's OK to bust your ass.* A lot of guys wanted to play like I did but were hesitant, because they didn't want to be called a showoff. I never cared if anyone called me that because I always played the same way. All they had to do was remember who my father was and how he played and they'd know what style I played.

Once you established yourself as a hard-nosed player, then you'd better not ever let up or you were going to hear it. You ran hard to first. You broke up a double play with whatever force or creativity was necessary. Your teammates knew it wasn't showboating. It was playing to win. I guess it was the same with the fans: If you were on their side, and all that extra stuff you did helped their team win, then they loved you. If you were on the other team, they probably loved to boo you. Before I went to Philadelphia, the fans there hated me. Oh, did they love to boo me in my years with the Cincinnati Reds! But they never once booed me when I was there playing for the Phillies.

The best part about Tampa was that my team was winning. We were eight games ahead by the middle of the season and everyone was hitting the ball. I was only one of three second basemen in the Reds organization turning some heads that year. I was named Player of the Month for May, and so were two other Reds prospects at my position: Tommy Harper, playing for Class B Topeka, and Cesar Tovar at Geneva, where I'd played the year before.

The same day I was named Player of the Month, June 10, I also hit inside-the-park home runs in each game of a doubleheader against the St. Petersburg Saints—and we won both games. At the end of June I was leading the league with a .381 average and also in runs scored, with sixty-nine.

Early in July, the Tarpons added a new first baseman to give us more power. His name was Lee May and he was big: six-foot-three and at least 200 pounds. He had a little wag at the plate before he swung the bat, and for the way he crushed the ball we called him the Big Bopper. He'd grown up in Birmingham, Alabama. Like me, he had a dad who played semipro baseball, and also like me, he had to decide between football and baseball. Lee turned down a football scholarship with the University of Nebraska to join the Reds organization and homered in one of his first games with the Tarpons that season.

I loved watching Lee bat, but his defense was a different story. That man could not catch a pop-up to save his life. I'm serious. He just couldn't do it. Every time a pop-up would drift down the first-base line, I'd be running to back him up as the second baseman, waiting for Lee to yell "I got it"—only that was never what he said.

"Who wants it?" he'd yell, staring up at that ball hovering somewhere above him.

So I'd have to run over and catch the ball, even if it came down over by the dugout! Lee would just stand there laughing. He knew his bat gave him his shot at the big leagues and his defense was never going to be anything to write home about. He had a short, compact swing, but still hit for power. Everybody liked Lee. He was easygoing and relaxed and never got mad.

As good as our team was that year in Tampa, winning ninety games in a 134-game season, we barely won the league championship. It came down to a five-game playoff against the Sarasota Sun Sox, and we won the fifth and deciding game 4–0. I doubled in one run and Lee May's two-run homer broke it open. I batted .300 in the playoffs and was one of four players from our team named to the

Florida State League all-star team. I finished the year with thirty triples, a league record that still stands, and an average of .331, second in the league.

I went home to Cincinnati and actually had a chance to practice with the Reds, which was a dream come true. Manager Fred Hutchinson didn't seem to be paying much attention to me, but that year he talked to a newspaper reporter.

"We had a chance to watch Pete during most of September," he told the *Dayton Daily News*. "He was out here every day working with us after his league closed around Labor Day—and he's a dandy."

Johnny Vander Meer was quoted in the same article, saying I had a shot at getting to the big leagues—and soon. "If desire and natural ability have anything to do with making it, Rose will come up in a hurry," he told sports editor Si Burick. "Maybe right away. He can field and he can hit and he can run and he's got so much enthusiasm, even when he gets a base on balls he races to first base as fast as he can."

Here's what Burick himself wrote in that October 1961 article:

"Who's going to play second base for Cincinnati next year? Now that Elio Chacon has been lost to the New York Mets, Don Blasingame survives as the squad's only man of major league experience at the position. But 'The Blazer' isn't the man he used to be and the spot obviously requires strengthening.

"Well, a kid who played on the Dayton sandlots as recently as the 1960 season, and who was in Class D pro ball this year, has a chance to make the almost impossible vault from the baseball depths to the big league in one year. . . . Pete Rose is now in Florida, where he'll be working in the Instructional League this fall. Between him and

Tommy Harper, a California bonus kid who spent his second pro season at Topeka in the Three-Eye league, the Reds may have second-base security for years to come."

What a long way I'd come in one year. Before then only my dad and I ever imagined me in the big leagues. Now the sports editor of a major American daily read by a lot of Reds fans was planting a seed with the organization about my future. Si Burick probably helped my cause more than he ever could have guessed.

CHAPTER 8

Instructional League

Even big league stars in those days were working off-season jobs, and if you were a farmhand like we all were, you knew you were going to be broke all the time. I didn't want to go back to loading and unloading freight cars for Railway Express out back of Crosley Field. Maybe the work would have done me more good, but your hope as a young player in those days was to get assigned to winter ball. I was one of the infielders chosen for the Florida State Instructional League—along with Tommy Harper, Tommy Helms, Mel Queen, and Miles McWilliams. Art Shamsky was one of the outfielders chosen. Just the top prospects would go to the instructional league.

I wasn't going to Florida to learn to hit. No one was worried about my bat. I was going to work more on my fielding, which was more than fine with me, so long as they kept the greenbacks coming. Every two weeks, they'd give us each an envelope with one hundred eighty bucks cash, and for players making what we did during the season, that was a decent bundle. Every game was a day game, so we'd be out there playing baseball all day every day, which sounded just about perfect to me.

You got out there early every morning and worked on things. You took a lot more ground balls, a lot more batting practice, and a lot more fielding practice. I was finally getting extra coaching, and nothing could have made me happier. I always loved the game of baseball and always wanted to learn every little thing I could about it, not just something to make me a better second baseman or better hitter or better base runner or better teammate, but anything that made me understand baseball better.

You had to learn the two or three ways to take the pivot on a double play. I knew where to go as a cutoff man, relaying throws from the outfield—that was easy. You worked on backhanding balls hit to your right, covering second, pop-ups—and on and on. If you just constantly, constantly, constantly took ground balls, you were going to get better at taking ground balls. Repetition was the key to mastery.

I didn't do anything different than what I always did, running to first base on every walk, stretching triples whenever I could, talking baseball with anyone and everyone at a mile a minute, practicing just as hard as I played. That was something I always did as long as I can remember. I always thought: *Even in practice, even in the minor leagues, people are watching me.* I wanted to be precise, hit the ball right, practice right, develop good habits and make them second nature.

"I don't think anybody has ever worked harder at being better than Pete Rose," Art Shamsky says now. "The word *No* was not in his vocabulary. He worked every day at getting better than whatever he was yesterday. He was always going to work hard to be one step better, and one step better."

We played Detroit late in October, and I doubled and had two singles. I also stole four bases. The headline in *The Tampa Tribune* was ROSE LEADS REDS OVER DETROIT. I liked the look of that. I aimed to see many more ROSE LEADS REDS headlines over the years.

We had a good team. The Reds' system was already loaded with talent, and it was one of the few organizations in baseball where you knew they were teaching the game right, instilling strong fundamentals in every player that came up. We were soon in first place in the Florida Instructional League, which didn't really matter, except winning always matters. Winning is a habit, and you learn how to win by winning.

The manager was Jack Cassini, the Reds scout who had briefly managed me in Geneva at the end of my first season in the Reds organization. His assistant was Hershell Freeman, a former relief pitcher for the Reds. In late November, two Cincinnati coaches, Jim Turner and Dick Sisler, came out to eye up the young talent on our team and came away impressed, talking up our big future.

"Only a couple of summers ago Pete Rose was an outfielder for the Lebanon club in the Dayton Double-A league," the *Dayton Daily News* wrote. "Cassini has played him sometimes at second base, sometimes at third. The latter spot is unfamiliar to him, but he wants to learn."

"This young man will find his natural spot in a hurry," Jim Turner told the Dayton paper. "I have no fears about saying he'll make a living at baseball, a very good living, and for a long time."

Cassini was a great base runner, and he helped me build on what I already knew. So much of it was about paying close attention. I wasn't the fastest guy, but I don't think there was ever a better base runner than me. You just had to have that attitude every time you were on first base that you knew you were going to make it over to third, any chance you got, no matter where the ball was hit. It was like when I hit a single, I always anticipated the outfielder might bobble it just a little and I'd be able to go to second. I was heading for second from the time I came out of the batter's box, and then if the guy fielded it cleanly, I'd take my big turn at first and go back.

I was leading off, getting a lot of hits, including triples—my specialty—and stealing bases. In mid-November my average was only .292, but we were in first place. I was leading the league in triples and Art Shamsky was first in home runs.

In late November, a scout told one newspaper reporter, "The Reds could get $150,000 for that kid's contract tomorrow."

You played hard all day and then you had some fun with the guys and relaxed. We had a routine. We'd play baseball all day, since in the instructional league you only play day games, then we'd get showered and changed and go have some food at a little drugstore lunch counter downtown. Then we'd go over to a tavern we liked where Tommy Helms would shoot pool. Mostly I'd just watch him, since shooting pool was never my thing—I'd learned that from Uncle Buddy years ago—but I always liked being around a pool table.

Interesting story: That was actually a gay bar, called Jimmy White's Tavern. Someone told us it was a friendly place, and we stopped by and liked it right away. We were just looking to unwind and relax, and at Jimmy White's, no one bothered us. The guys there made for good friends, and they treated us like kings. We watched out for them. If someone came in, trying to make trouble, they got one look at me and Tommy and realized they'd be better off moving on. Guys didn't come in and tease them about being gay when we were around. We would police up the area if somebody tried to be a smartass.

The bar, originally known as Jimmy White's La Concha Bar and Tavern, had a colorful history. According to a 1955 article in the *Tampa Times*, "The tavern was noted as a hangout for jazz addicts, being induced to assemble at the tavern on Sunday afternoons by special 'jam sessions.'"

I found out later that the FBI actually had the place under surveillance around the time we used to hang out there. In fact, an October 7, 1961, FBI report on Florida night spots named Jimmy White's Tavern as among the "hangouts for homosexuals" the Bureau had been monitoring.

We went to a gay wedding one night at Jimmy White's. Like I said, we were there every night, and we had nothing against two gay people wanting to get married to each other. We didn't really think about it much, to be honest. These were our friends at the time and that was a big event for them. This was in the backroom at Jimmy White's, only about twenty people were there, including me and Tommy.

After the ceremony they brought out a wedding cake and guess what was on top of that cake? A big dick! We couldn't get over that: a big dick right there on the top of the cake.

I even dated a girl who worked there. She wasn't gay. She was a star in the circus, doing acrobatics, and she was unbelievable, a fox like that who could move her body the way she did. There are a lot of pictures online from Jimmy White's in those years, showing lesbians and cross-dressers.

It was different, that's for sure, but for us it was a kind of retreat from the usual grind, a great way to unwind after another long day of busting our butts on the baseball field, so we could get ready for another day. Part of working hard is knowing how to unwind a little. Not much, but a little.

I was going to be tightly wound no matter what I did. Johnny Vander Meer told *Cincinnati Enquirer* sports columnist Lou Smith that I reminded him of Pepper Martin, the longtime St. Louis Cardinal from Oklahoma who was known as the Wild Horse of the Osage. He wasn't big, maybe five-seven, but he would slide headfirst, and when I was young my dad and I decided I'd slide headfirst, too. That way you never lost sight of the ball and could avoid the tag. "He's got more stomach than a parachute jumper," Vander Meer told the columnist on the day I was named "Player of the Year" for the Florida State League. I just kept doing what I was doing.

On December 11, I scored the winning run against Detroit on a play that showed the power of alert base-running to swing a game. As the *Tampa Tribune* reported, "Rose singled and stole second, then raced all the way home on two subsequent throwing errors."

The season ended, and it was time to go back to Cincinnati for the holidays. The cover of the *Tampa Tribune* sports section carried an interesting article on New Year's Eve. Would you believe this? I was one of eighteen athletes nominated as the top professional athlete in the Tampa area. Considering I only played there for a small part of the year, that was quite an honor. And I was being nominated with people like Reds pitcher Joey Jay, who was coming off a 21–10 season and helped the Reds to their first National League pennant in twenty years, and Al Lopez, manager of the Chicago White Sox. It was a diverse list, with golfers, bowlers, wrestlers, you name it. But being a car guy the way I was, my favorite part was seeing my name on the same list as dragster driver Art Malone, who held the closed-track speed record of 182 miles per hour, and, of course, "Big Daddy" Don Garlits.

CHAPTER 9

Macon

I proved my uncle Buddy right. He'd insisted to the Reds organization back when I was a high school kid that I was going to grow, and even after I'd grown a couple more inches in the off-season before playing in Tampa, he kept telling them I had more growing to do. By the time I reported to spring training in Florida in early 1962, headed for the Class A Macon Peaches in the South Atlantic League, I had grown another couple inches and put on some more muscle. I was five-eleven, 185 pounds, and I still played the game as hard as I could. I had more energy than anyone else around and I had to let that energy out all the time.

"Pete Rose is a physical freak," Tommy Harper said later. "I've never seen a guy with his energy. He never gets tired. He jumps out of bed in the morning, goes into his hitting stance, and takes batting practice in the hotel room with an imaginary bat. I'm just lying there, rubbing my eyes, wishing I could go back to sleep for a couple more hours!"

I lucked out again on getting a great manager that year in Dave

Bristol. He was young for a manager, only twenty-nine that season, but he was already in his sixth year managing. He had a future, everyone knew, and he was a great guy. He'd get in fights all the time, but he'd never win one. That never stopped him from getting in another fight. He'd never back down from one. It was just the way it was. He was a fucking terror. He still is. I love Dave Bristol.

I'll never forget one time when we were playing in Macon. In those days in the minor leagues you had a pitching coach, a first-base coach, and the manager. That was it, so consequently the manager would coach third base during the game. Dave was out there coaching third base and got into an altercation with Elmo Plaskett, the catcher for Asheville. We all got to the scene, and Elmo took off his mask and swung it and hit Dave right in the face with it. Now Dave's nose is bleeding. Blood is squirting out of his fucking eye. He's lying on the ground, and we're all gathered around him. Suddenly he hopped up and went into a fighter's stance.

"All right, Elmo, you had enough?" he said. "Or do you want some more?"

Another time, Dave took the lineup cards up to home plate just before a game. He had been kicked out the night before, and as he walked up with the lineup cards, he handed the opposing manager a tube of Vaseline.

"I got fucked last night," he said. "You get ready to get fucked tonight."

That was enough for the umpire.

"Get *out* of here!"

They kicked him out of the game before it even started! That was Dave.

The Sally League, as it was called, had eight teams, including the Knoxville (Tennessee) Smokies, Greenville (South Carolina) Spinners, Asheville (North Carolina) Tourists, and several teams in Georgia. For our road games we traveled by three station wagons. We might have a two-and-a-half-hour ride over to Augusta, for example.

We had a great double-play combination in me and shortstop Tommy Helms, who had an even better year at the plate in Macon than I did. He and I were just getting to know each other that year. "Here was a guy who hustled all the time—even in spring training— nonstop," Tommy remembers about me. "A lot of people were calling him a hot dog and all that stuff, and that's just the way he was. He ran everything out. He was a guy who stuck out."

We didn't have many black players on our team that season in Macon, but on the road they had to ride with Dave Bristol in station wagon No. 1, just in case they got pulled over. That was how it was in the South. You wanted the top guy there to look out for them. We were playing games in Savannah and Augusta, and what I remember more about that year than anything was going to those ballparks and seeing signs on the restrooms telling you one was WHITE ONLY and one was COLORED ONLY.

I'd never seen that before. Not where I grew up. I just couldn't comprehend what I was seeing with those signs. My black teammates had always been my friends, going back to high school. To this day I never do look at the color of a guy's skin. I never did care about that.

Art Shamsky and I would ride together all the way in the back of one of the station wagons, facing the car behind us with our feet out the back window. That was the only way we could get comfortable. Some of those trips were pretty long. If you were driving from

Macon, Georgia, to Portsmouth, Virginia, that's more than six hundred miles. Nine hours in the back of one of those station wagons was more than enough to make us go a little stir crazy. Just to break up the monotony, we'd think up gags. One time I climbed out the back window, barreling down the highway at sixty-five miles per hour, climbed up onto the luggage rack on the roof, and pulled myself all the way forward to the windshield and slapped a hand down there. The driver, a pitcher named Marv Fodor, about messed his pants!

Late that April, we had a game in Greenville, South Carolina, and I started the night 0 for 2. Dave Bristol always talked about this game. A lot of guys when they start out 0 for 2, they slip into thinking it's just not their night. They'd try to get a hit, just to avoid an O-fer, but they were already kind of wishing the night was over. That was never my style.

"Pete was the greediest player I ever had," Bristol would say years later, "and that's not a knock."

I always saw myself getting more hits, and that night, I figured I still had some time. We had twenty-eight hits as a team that night, and I had six of them, including a two-run homer and a triple. On a night when I started 0 for 2, I went 6 for 8 with six RBIs. We won 32–5 and knocked around everyone they sent out there.

As the local paper put it, "Greenville used seven 'pitchers' during the evening, including two infielders and a catcher. None had any success against the Macon assault."

I was enjoying myself, and I didn't mind if people knew it. I'd used my signing bonus to buy a fuel-injected Corvette, light green on the side, with GREEN BEAN written on it. That was what the previous owner had painted on there. He'd drag it every Sunday. That was a sweet ride, 283 horsepower, and I got her up to 102 one time. My mother drove it for me from Cincinnati to Knoxville, Tennessee, where we had a game, and then I drove it back to Macon from there, a three-hour drive. I remember Tommy Helms was with me and we headed right down I-75, curving around the Chattahoochee National Forest.

Not long after we crossed into Georgia, I saw lights flashing behind me. I wasn't hardly speeding, maybe going 70 in a 55 zone, something like that. The local sheriff pulled us over and sauntered up to the car. He was nice and all, but he insisted we follow him back to the station. We got there and went before the justice of the peace or whatever he was. It was about two o'clock in the morning, so the place was cleared out.

"Empty your pockets," he said.

Tommy and I dug out everything we had, which amounted to five dollars and ninety cents between us.

"Now get the fuck out of here," he said.

That was our fine. He'd taken every cent we had! Good thing we'd just gassed up the Corvette so we could drive the 150 miles back to Macon. Still, I was as hot as a match about the whole thing.

Some of my teammates still didn't know what to make of me. They figured I was getting some breaks because I was a Cincinnati kid, born and raised, a good story for the hometown fans. Maybe there was something to that. I'd been a Reds fan my whole life.

One of my roommates that season was Mel Queen, whose dad had pitched for the Yankees. Mel was born in New York but grew up in California, where his dad was playing in the Pacific Coast League.

"I roomed with him for a while, and I think he had more energy than anyone else has ever had playing a particular sport," Mel said later. "Maybe Walter Payton had the same thing, and maybe Michael Jordan, for their sports. Pete had this for baseball. He lived and died baseball."

He got that right. The best thing about that season playing for Macon was, like the year before, we had a good team. The Greenville paper ran an article that May quoting Ernie White, manager of the Augusta Yankees, on our success. At the time we were on pace to win a record 110 games or more. "They're doing it on hustle," he told the paper.

"The spark of Macon seems to be second baseman Pete Rose, everyone agrees," Jim Anderson wrote. "'He can get down to first faster than anyone else in the league,' said Ernie. And Rose, being called a major league prospect, is a fiery competitor who instills the desire to win in his teammates. He's an Eddie Stanky who can hit and field better than Stanky."

Tommy Helms had a lot to do with our success as well. He was leading the league in hitting and I was leading in runs scored. I'd hit .331 the year before and was near that in June, lifting my average to .323 by late in the month. Tommy did lead the league in hits, but he finished the season third in the league with a .340 average, behind Elmo Plaskett and Tony Oliva. I finished with a league-high 136 runs scored, a team record, and tied for fourth in batting with an average of .330. I also led the league in triples with seventeen, meaning that over my first two full seasons in professional baseball I'd hit forty-seven triples.

We finished the regular season in third place, then took three in a row from first-place Savannah in the semifinals and three of four from Knoxville. We won the championship with a 21–3 rout at our home field in Macon, Luther Williams Park, and it was my grand slam that broke it open. Mel Queen, Art Shamsky, Tommy Helms, and I all had homers.

"Rose's was the one that really mattered, though," the *Asheville Citizen-Times* reported. "The fiery second sacker broke up what had been a torrid mound duel between Macon's Harvey Alex and Knoxville's Bill Faul when he lined one over the fence in right center at the 360-foot mark in the bottom of the sixth with the bases loaded. . . . After Rose's belt, the visitors fell apart and the other circuit blows were just so much icing on the cake."

Tommy and I were voted to the league's all-star team, and were both chosen to go to the Florida Instructional League, along with Art Shamsky. I was batting .346 at the time of the winter league all-star game and was selected for the team. Manager Don Heffner said I was one of six on the team he figured were about ready for the big leagues. They called me cocky, but I was just being honest when I talked to a *Cincinnati Enquirer* reporter down in Florida. He wanted to know if I thought I was going to be the Reds' second baseman the next year. I figured I'd give him some good material for his article.

"It all depends on Don Blasingame," I told him. "I'm going to be on his heels."

I said it with a smile, but still, it was brash. I couldn't be too surprised when the reporter wrote, "Rose has been a cocky one ever since he broke in with the Class D Tampa Tarpons in the Florida State League. He once told the Tarpons' public address announcer, 'Stick with me and we'll go to the majors together.'"

CHAPTER 10

Straight to the Bigs

To me there was only one reason to go to spring training: to try to make the Cincinnati Reds. I was told that was out of the question. I was told that I had absolutely no shot at making the big league team at that time. The organization had me projected going to San Diego to play Triple-A ball to start the 1963 season and continue my development. I wasn't so sure about that. I planned to bust my ass in Tampa that spring and see if I couldn't make them change those plans.

What I didn't know at the time was that Fred Hutchinson, the Reds' manager, had been following my progress in the instructional league. He liked what he saw of me.

"As soon as Hutch saw Pete play, he fell in love with him," *Cincinnati Post* beat writer Earl Lawson remembered later. "At the winter meetings that year, he told me, 'If I had any guts, I'd stick Rose at second base and just leave him there.'"

That's what the winter meetings were for, throwing ideas out there. I may have had a receptive audience in Hutch, but I'd have to earn my future by showing what I could do during spring training.

Tommy Helms was just as much an up-and-comer as me at that point and might have had an edge on me, but he was out of the picture. We were being asked to play for almost no money back in those days, at least compared to how it was later in my career. Tommy decided to hold out. "I had just hit .340, and back then they didn't give raises," he remembered. "I think they wanted to give me a twenty-five-dollar-a-month raise. I didn't think I could make it on $450 a month."

Baseball was my life. I gave everything to it. So I always felt like I belonged and let it show, even if I was a fresh-faced rook who ought to have piped down a little. I remember that getting under the skin of veterans like John Edwards, the catcher, a big guy at six-foot-four, 220 or so. He was one of the guys who made sure to keep me in my place as a twenty-one-year-old with no time in the majors up to then.

One day I was stepping up to bat and just kept taking practice swings, as many as I needed. Edwards watched me, looking more annoyed by the second.

"Can't you count?" he asked me.

I didn't miss a beat.

"No, I never got to go to Kent State like you," I shot right back.

So what if he went to Ohio State at Columbus, not Kent State? What was the difference?

Veteran pitcher Bill Henry got one look at my brush cut and cracked, "Who ever heard of a superstar with a flat top?" and everyone laughed.

It was the same with veteran New York Yankees Whitey Ford and Mickey Mantle. They saw me take off running for first after earning a walk that spring.

"Hey," Whitey said to the Mick sarcastically, slapping him on the shoulder. "Check out Charlie Hustle."

In those days, you put "Charlie" in front of a lot of things. My attitude was: If they want to call me Charlie Hustle, so much the better. It shows I've got their attention.

On a rainy March 20 in Tampa, we beat Minnesota to hit .500 for the first time in weeks in Grapefruit League play. "Former Western Hills Hi star Pete Rose continued to impress manager Hutchinson with his brilliant all-around play," *Cincinnati Enquirer* sports editor Lou Smith wrote the next day. "Rose thrilled the handful of spectators by turning an ordinary single into a double."

The article went on: "When questioned about the current status of Pete Rose, Hutch said, 'He's having a helluva spring. As of now I'd have to say he's on our roster. There isn't anything he hasn't done well so far.'"

Even so, Lou Smith was betting against me. "It is still this observer's opinion that Pete, who played for the Macon club of the Sally League last season, will do most of his second basing this season for San Diego, the Reds' No. 1 farm club of the Pacific Coast League," he wrote.

Si Burick, sports editor of the *Dayton Daily News*, disagreed. Writing that weekend, when I was down in Mexico City with some of the team for three exhibition games, he talked me up in an article with the headline PETE ROSE MOST EXCITING PLAYER IN REDS' SPRING TRAINING CAMP. He not only predicted I would make the big jump and start the season with the Cincinnati Reds, but he added: "He might even open the season at second base ahead of the veteran Don Blasingame, who had an excellent 1962 season. . . .

"He gives the club added speed, enthusiasm, drive. He wants to play . . . and was picked as the second baseman on the seventeen-man squad Fred Hutchinson took to Mexico City this weekend. Hutch has become so fond of the youngster he doesn't want to let him out of his sight. Or so it seems."

We flew from Miami to Mexico City, and that was my first time leaving the country. Only some of the players made that trip, and fortunately for me Frank Robinson was one of them. He was not only a great player, he was a great teacher of the game, which was why he would go on to be such a good manager, the first African American manager in Major League Baseball.

Frank knew that when he talked baseball, I always listened, and he rewarded me with a steady stream of advice. He would guide me through how to approach a new pitcher, point by point. Like when we went up against the Cardinals that year in spring training, facing Curt Simmons, he broke him down for me, saying, "He'll jam you and make you lean outside and then come back. He's a little faster than he looks." Now, some of that advice Frank gave worked a lot better for him than it did for anyone else. You could be a smarter hitter and still not be Frank Robinson up there. But talking to Frank opened up whole new worlds of thinking for me and made me vow that every year I played baseball in the big leagues, I'd find ways to learn more and become a smarter hitter.

At the start of April, still in Florida, Hutchinson was asked about having said at the winter meetings that if he had any "guts" he'd put me on second base for the season. He answered, "No comment," and smiled. I was smiling, too.

"I thought training with the Reds would be the greatest thing in the world, and it was the first few weeks," I told reporters. "Now I feel like I'm one of them."

Our last game of spring training was against the New York Mets, managed by Casey Stengel, and I had myself a pretty good game. I had a couple hits and scored three runs, and we won 5–0 to wrap up our Grapefruit League season on April 3. Everyone seemed to assume afterward that I'd made the team, but I wasn't going to assume anything.

Hutch pulled his coaching staff together for a meeting to discuss final cuts. They liked my defense and the way I played the game, but they were worried I wasn't ready to hit big league pitching.

"Do any of you think we'd hurt our chances by giving him a trial, and is there any of you who feels he hasn't earned it?" Hutchinson asked his coaches.

No one raised any objections. I was breaking camp with the team. I was going to the big leagues.

My first game was our home opener, which was Opening Day for all of baseball back then, given Cincinnati's status as the cradle of professional baseball. I signed my first contract two or three hours before that game.

I walked into the clubhouse after that, and I'll never forget the sight of a crisp, clean Reds uniform with number 14 on the back. All spring I'd been number 27, but that was a spring-training number.

Now I was part of the big league team and I had a big league number.

I wasn't nervous at all before the game until a photographer from the *Cincinnati Enquirer* approached me.

"Can I get a picture with your mom and dad?" he asked me.

I said sure. So they brought my mom and dad down the runway for a picture, and that kind of woke me up. Or I think I was awake? I'm not sure. The *Louisville Courier-Journal* published a picture of me running out from the Reds' dugout at the start of the game on April 8, 1963. The headline at the top of the page was ROOKIE PETE ROSE SPENDS A BUSY FIRST DAY IN REDS' LINEUP. I'm grinning so wide and look so young in that picture, you'd think it was my birthday.

Another thing you notice in the picture is, as I'm running out, the player to my right, also running, is right fielder Vada Pinson, and on my left, about to start an easy run, is the great Frank Robinson, our left fielder. The three of us were three-quarters of the top of the order, with manager Fred Hutchinson putting me in the two hole, Vada hitting third, and Frank batting cleanup. Without those two, my rookie year would have been a whole lot different.

They say you always remember your first time, and I'll never forget my first major league at bat. The mood in the stands that day was really exciting; there was an electricity in the air that you felt down on the field, with 28,896 fans all waiting for something to happen. I stepped into the box in the first inning against the Pirates' big right-hander, Earl Francis, and I was so scared, I don't think I could have swung even if he'd thrown it right down the middle. He never did! He walked me on four pitches and I did what I always do: I took off at a dead run down to first base.

Let them call me Charlie Hustle all they want. I was going to play the game the way my daddy taught me to play the game. I came around to score when Frank Robinson drilled a home run to left field. I flew down from third base and touched home plate—the first run of the season for the Reds, and the first run out of 2,165 I'd score in my career.

It was when I stepped on home plate and headed into the dugout that I realized for the first time: *I'm playing second base for the Cincinnati Reds.* Ever since I was a little boy, I wanted to play second base for the Cincinnati Reds, and now that dream had come true. The feeling was unbelievable, even if I didn't get a hit that night.

I also turned three double plays at second and we won the game, which was what mattered most to me. Earl Ruby, *Louisville Courier-Journal* columnist, had some fun the next day writing about me, local boy makes good and all that. The headline was PETE "CHARLEY HUS- TLE" ROSE OF REDS RUNS EVEN WHEN HE "WALKS" TO FIRST BASE.

"Pete learned his baseball from his dad, an old time boxer, who believed there was more money and less chance for injury on the diamond than in the ring," Earl wrote. "He taught his son to switch hit and to hustle. 'Just remember,' he told Pete over and over. 'You've got to hit the ball and also be on the ball.' Pete hustles so much that he runs to first base like an Olympic dash man even when he draws a walk. And he tries mightily with the bat from both sides of the plate."

I'd talked to sports reporters before and after the game. I never minded that part of being a ballplayer. They've got a job to do, like anyone else, and I usually enjoyed the back-and-forth. As a brand-new rookie, I was just trying to be honest and take things as they came.

We played one game at home and then were flying to Philadelphia for a series against the Phillies at Connie Mack Stadium, the former Shibe Park, which had opened back in 1909 as the first stadium in baseball made of concrete and steel. One of the sportswriters asked me if I'd ever been to Connie Mack Stadium before, and I smiled and said: "You name a park in the league and I'll tell you I've never been there." Like I said, just being honest.

You know what might have been the best part of that day? I showered after the game and got dressed and did my interviews and walked out of the clubhouse, going down to the team bus. My dad was on one side, my mom on the other, my little brother David, friends from Cincinnati—all those years my dad and I would come here and watch players come out of the clubhouse, heading for a team bus, and now I was with the Reds, and my dad got to enjoy seeing his son get on that bus and ride off with the whole team.

We got to the airport and, I'm not going to lie, I was pretty amped up. I was a long ways from getting used to flying. I hurried off to go buy some candy bars and a few packs of gum, then started thinking maybe I'd miss the plane if I didn't hurry, so I ran through the gate and down onto the tarmac, walked behind the tail of the DC-7, and then half ran up the ramp and onto the plane. I was still smiling when Frank Robinson gave me the news.

"You've got to help serve dinner," Frank told me. "I usually help, but I want to play cards."

I thought he was kidding me at first. He was not. Gordy Coleman and I served all the guys steaks, and went around afterward with a pot of coffee, filling up everyone's cups. Finally I grabbed a steak for myself and sat down next to Vada Pinson and started eating. I was hungry.

"How did you really feel before the game?" someone asked me.

"If he says he wasn't nervous, don't you believe him," Vada answered for me. "I know, I was young myself once."

"Sure, I was nervous, but not scared," I said. "There's a difference."

PART 3

BECOMING PETE ROSE

CHAPTER II

Frank and Vada

I scored the Reds' first run of the 1963 season in my first game in the major leagues, but I had to sweat it out before I could get my first big league hit. I was 0-for-3 on Opening Day against the Pirates, and then 0 for 4 in both games in Philadelphia, then after a couple days off we were back home at Crosley Field for a game against Pittsburgh. It was cold, 57 degrees at game time, and Pirates starter Bob Friend ran my streak to 0 for 12 early in the game. My next time up, he hit me, so I sprinted on down to first base, still 0 for 12.

I had one more shot at him in the eighth inning. He pitched me away and I went with the pitch, driving the ball down the left-field line. I didn't stand and watch it. I took off running and was thinking triple all the way. What else would I be thinking? I'd made my name in the minor leagues as the king of the triple, so I thought that was kind of ironic, getting all that notoriety for my triples in the minor leagues and now my first major league hit was a triple. I'd have been happy to stand out there awhile and enjoy the feeling, but Vada singled me home straightaway, and Frank followed with another home run. We lost anyway. The next day was my twenty-second birthday, so that triple was a mighty fine birthday present.

By then I knew where I stood with most of the veterans on the team, which was nowhere. They wanted nothing to do with me. They'd gone to spring training thinking that Don Blasingame, a pretty good hitter for the Reds the year before, would be back at second base. Two years earlier, he'd been a part of the Reds team that made it all the way to the World Series, losing to the Yankees in five games. They had a group of guys from that World Series team that liked playing together and wanted to get back to the series again and win it together, guys like Gordy Coleman, Gene Freeze, Eddie Kasco, and Johnny Edwards. They were good guys, but they were real cliquish. If you were on the outs with them, you were really on the outs.

So we open the season in Cincinnati, and the manager, Fred Hutchinson, takes a brash rookie—me—and replaces their guy in the Opening Day lineup. Of course they resented me! None of those veterans thought much of me or my style. They didn't like the way I'd caught Hutch's eye. They didn't like all the publicity I was getting as a local kid who'd hit .330 two years in the minors. They didn't like me running to first base every chance I had or running my mouth off, and you know what? I just didn't care. I was having the time of my life, playing for my hometown team, and I figured I might as well enjoy it. But I had a lot to learn—and they weren't going to teach me.

I stopped in at the offices of the *Cincinnati Enquirer* a week into the season. I'd played all six games at second base up until then, and I overheard an argument—so of course I stepped right into the middle of that.

Here's how it was published in the paper under the headline A
ROSE BY ANY OTHER NAME—WOULD BE LESS INTERESTED:

"'I don't know why,' argued the Reds' fan who happened into a
downtown debating parlor at which The Enquirer Sports Department usually presides, 'Hutch doesn't bench that kid Rose. He can't
hit and Hutch should go with Blasingame, who does hit and has the
experience.'

"'Because the kid has speed,' volunteered the young intruder,
sitting within earshot.

"'Whose speed?' exploded the fan, upset by the interruption.

"'MY speed,' shot back the neatly dressed intruder, whose working clothes are the Reds' flannels on which No. 14 is affixed.

"Number 14 belongs to Pete Rose."

But then in our seventh game of the season, at home against the
Mets, Blasingame was starting at second again and I was on the bench.
The next day's *Enquirer* carried this update from Lou Smith: "Rookies Pete Rose and Tommy Harper were out of the starting lineup in
the final game with the Mets. And the guessing now is that the two
highly touted rookies will be optioned to San Diego before the Reds
return from their first West Coast trip a week from next Monday."

A couple days later, the reporters asked Hutch if Tommy Harper
and I were about to be sent down. "No decision has been made on
either one," he said.

He kept telling reporters he didn't know, and would have to talk
to the owner, Bill DeWitt, who'd started out as a protégé of Branch
Rickey's in St. Louis and bought control of the Reds before the 1962
season. I was lucky through it all that I had friends like Frank Robinson and Vada Pinson, who helped keep my head on straight and just

focused on what I could control, which was my own approach to the game. One thing you can never do as a ballplayer is worry about what might happen.

There was always going to be trade talk—Bill DeWitt would eventually trade Frank himself, one of the great players in the history of the game—and rumors about players being sent down. In those days, if you didn't do the job, then you could count on being sent down, because there were only eight teams. But until any of it happened, you were better off ignoring the rumors. Just keep yourself ready and then, when you get another chance, jump on it.

We flew down to Houston for a three-game series with the Colt .45s, and that Saturday both Tommy Harper and I were back in the lineup and I was batting second again. I went 1 for 3 and we won to snap a losing streak, but in the eighth inning I was hit in the head by a throw and was dazed enough that I had to lie there a few minutes. Nowadays they might have made me take time off, but I was back in the lineup the next day and went on a tear, including my first major league homer against the Cardinals on May 3. By mid-May I was hitting .338 since my return to the starting lineup.

"Pete was always my good friend," Harper said later. "Not my white friend, my friend. Those first years in the major leagues he was always chirping on me, encouraging me: 'C'mon, Harp, c'mon Harp!' He would say 'We're going to do this' and 'We're going to do that,' they're not going to be able to send us back down. It was always 'we, we, we' with Pete. It wasn't 'I.'"

Frank and Vada kind of adopted me that year and taught me how to be a big leaguer. They saw something in me that the other guys couldn't. They treated me like I was one of the guys. They were the only ones on that team who really treated me like a teammate at that time, them and Jesse Gonder, a catcher, also from Oakland, California, like they were.

"We were upset, too; we couldn't understand why Blasingame was being edged out," Vada said later. "But Frank and I had been through plenty of discrimination ourselves—having to board with black families in spring training because we couldn't stay in the team hotel, being barred from certain restaurants. The way Pete was being treated was not something we were going to go for. It upset me. He was a rookie, untried. But he had a uniform on, he was a teammate, and we were trying to win. The way I was raised was to treat people as human beings, fellow human beings. I think that's all we did with Pete."

"We accepted him for what he was," Frank said later. "They called him a hot dog for trying to do things he couldn't. We admired him for laboring beyond his skills. They resented him for taking one of their friends' jobs. Well, we could all relate to that. Nobody had to show him how to hit, but they wouldn't even show him how to be a major leaguer. So we did."

What I cared about was how someone played the game of baseball, and Frank Robinson played the game with as much intensity and commitment as I did. They called him "the black Ty Cobb," but Frank couldn't be compared to anyone. He had a style all his own. He and Vada were both such polished and all-around players, I could talk baseball with them all day long, which was what I did. That really got under the skin of the white veterans on the team, the way we'd talk and talk and talk. I might even shine Frank's shoes while we were talking. Why not? I was a rook.

I was finally summoned for a meeting in the Reds' front office to see Phil Seghi. I had no idea what it could be about. This was midseason, and by then I was already getting some consideration for Rookie of the Year. I didn't think he was shipping me out, but what else could be on his mind?

"You've got to quit hanging around with the black players so much," Phil Seghi told me.

I just stared at him.

"What?" I said.

I couldn't believe it. Phil was a friend of Uncle Buddy's, and he only wanted what was best for me. He was passing along what others were saying, and I knew that. It came from the upper echelon. There was enough racism that some people in Cincinnati didn't like the idea of me fraternizing with Frank and Vada and Jesse Gonder, but I couldn't have cared less if that bothered anyone.

"Let me tell you why I hang around with Frank and Vada and Jesse, because they're the only three on the fucking team that treat me like I'm a fucking teammate," I told him.

And you know what I did different after that? Not a damn thing. I was never used to anything like that. I'm not worried about what color your skin is. I'm worried about if you can get on base or knock me in. Frank and Vada weren't doing anything illegal. You know what they were doing? Hitting behind me, Vada second and Frank third.

The Reds unloaded Blasingame in the middle of the season. I'd won the competition. He was thirty-one years old by then and had batted just .161 in eighteen games. He ended up with the Washington Senators, who sent back a six-foot-four right-handed pitcher named Jim Coates, who'd been traded by the Yankees earlier that year.

We headed to San Francisco for more games with the Giants in June and again in August, and Frank and Vada invited me to come along with them to Oakland to see where they grew up. So many good ballplayers were from Oakland, Frank and Vada and Jesse Gondor and so many others. I enjoyed being with them on their home turf. They took me to a place called the Showcase Lounge, a nightclub that booked acts like Little Junior Parker, Bobby Blue Bland, Cal Tjader, and B. B. King. I walked into this place and I'm one of the only white guys in there out of hundreds of clubgoers, but because I was with Frank and Vada, I was treated like a king.

We were in Chicago for three games at Wrigley Field in September, and the team had me rooming with Jim Coates, the pitcher we'd added in exchange for Don Blasingame. Vada and I went out to eat after the game. Frank Robinson was not on that road trip, since he'd been badly spiked by Mets second baseman Ron Hunt and had a deep gash on his left arm.

Vada and I were enjoying ourselves, and by the time we got back to the hotel, it was just after midnight. That was curfew. Vada and I went up to the floor where our rooms were, and I tried to open the door to my room and I couldn't. Coates had put the fucking chain on the door! Which I couldn't understand—even if he's got a girl in there, I've still got to sleep, don't I? He was an ass, but he was also a veteran, and I wasn't about to bang on the door and wake him up. I turned to Vada.

"Come on, sleep in Frank's bed," he said. "You won't bother nobody. We've got two beds in the room."

So that was what I did. We walked down to Vada's room, and I got a good night of sleep in Frank's bed.

"Do you want room service?" Vada asked me the next morning.

"What?"

"Room service."

I stared at him for a minute. That was a new one on me. Service to your room? That sounded great.

"Yeah, sure," I said.

I couldn't get over it. A little while later there was a knock on the door and someone wheeled in a little cart with a full breakfast for each of us, ham and eggs and coffee. There might even have been orange juice. That was my first room service. It cost $12.75, I'll never forget, and Vada picked up the tab.

"Now go down and change your clothes and let's go to the ballpark," he said.

As I recall, we went out that day and beat the Cubs, 8–4, and Vada went 2 for 5 with a home run and four RBIs. Coates was not involved.

I even saw Frank and Vada in the off-season. I never played basketball in high school, but I liked the sport, and when I became a professional baseball player, I found that basketball was a great way to stay in shape and have some fun in the winter. So I had my own basketball team that would travel around and play different teams of coaches and teachers, you name it. They'd sell out and raise some money and share a little with us. We were all ballplayers on my team. I had Johnny Bench and Lee May. And Frank Robinson and Vada Pinson would play with the team.

One time we had a game in Portsmouth, Virginia, and I rode with Frank and Vada. After the game I collected our share, and on the way home we stopped at Big Boy to get some food. I took the opportunity to pull out the cash and start counting it out, one for you, one for you, one for me. The next thing I know, someone had called the cops on us. They showed up and saw two African Americans with a pile of cash in front of them and thought we must have robbed a bank.

"Listen, this is Frank Robinson," I told the cops, drawing out the syllables to make my point. "This is one of the greatest baseball players ever!"

I had to keep working on them, explaining that we'd just played a basketball game in Portsmouth, but once they knew who we all were, everything was fine. We were all laughing about the misunderstanding, but it wasn't funny.

I felt something in common with my black teammates. Maybe it had to do with having people underestimate us or look down on us. But mainly I just liked the conversation. I loved talking baseball, especially talking hitting, and Frank and Vada knew their stuff.

A few years later, when Dusty Baker and Ralph Garr came into the league and were both playing for the Atlanta Braves, along with Hank Aaron, I got to know the two of them. I even took them out to lunch one time in Cincinnati. That was not something I did very often, take opposing players out for a meal, but they were bright, young players who were always talking to me at the ballpark about hitting. I knew they were staying at the Terrace Plaza Hotel downtown, so we met near there. They were both really talented players, and dedicated to the game.

Now, a funny thing about that lunch was, I had a lot of clothes then and I remembered what it was like as a young player, just scraping by on your meal money. So I offered Ralph and Dusty some of my suits.

"They were leisure suits," Dusty says now.

Exactly, real nice suits.

CHAPTER 12

Rookie of the Year

Sure I wanted to be Rookie of the Year. Didn't everyone who ever stepped on a baseball field want to be Rookie of the Year? It wasn't my number one goal—that was winning the World Series. And being a great teammate. And always playing as hard as I could. I guess that's more than one goal, but you get my point. For me, in 1963, Rookie of the Year was one more way to give myself a kick in the pants and push myself always to give more, do more, player harder, play better. And then, when over the course of the season I actually went out and did those things, it started to feel like I'd earned the recognition.

By the midpoint of my first big league season, I'd established myself as the Reds' everyday second baseman and earned some respect around the league. Leonard Koppett noted in his *New York Times* National League midseason report that I had already positioned myself as a Rookie of the Year candidate. "Three rookies have proved themselves so far: Ron Hunt, the second baseman of the Mets; Pete Rose, the second baseman of Cincinnati; and Tim McCarver, the catcher of the Cardinals. All have played well in the field as well as hit, and have won regular jobs."

Having shown I belonged, I could settle in enough to take in what I was seeing and hearing, and do my best to learn from it. I did that talking baseball every day with Frank Robinson and Vada Pinson, and I learned from Hutch and the coaches, too. But the education I was after was broader than learning the double-play pivot on defense or the fine points of opposite-field hitting. I wanted to soak up as much baseball as I could: baseball history, baseball lore, baseball color. For that I was lucky to have as a resource the great former Yankees pitcher Waite Hoyt, whose Reds broadcasts I'd grown up listening to the way others focus on a church sermon. Now I could sit next to him on the airplane and hear his stories firsthand.

Cincinnati loved Waite so much, we might have been the only fans around who actually rooted for rain delays, because then we could listen to Waite tell stories for as long as it took. He had a knack for telling stories, and they were always interesting and insightful. I tried to pump him for stories when I was a rookie and he actually tolerated my questions. I think I reminded him of an old-time ballplayer.

Me being the type of player I was and the type of baseball fan I was, I could listen to his stories all day, especially if he talked about Babe Ruth, his former teammate on both the Boston Red Sox and New York Yankees. Everyone always talked about the 1927 Yankees as maybe the best baseball team ever. Waite went 22–7 for the Yankees that season, tying him for the league lead. This was a man who pitched in the major league for twenty-one seasons.

Waite told me on one of those flights that one time he got into a fight with Babe, because evidently Babe messed up a ball in center field that cost Waite his twentieth win. The two of them got into a scuffle in the dugout and they didn't talk for a year, but he loved Babe. He told me about one time in Chicago when he was in a speakeasy with the Babe.

Babe had a cigar going, and plenty of beer. "I wanna meet the big guy," he said to the bartender.

About five minutes later a couple limos pull up outside and a few tough-looking characters came into the speakeasy.

"Who wants to meet the big guy?" they asked.

"I do!" Babe said.

"Follow us," they said.

Once Babe and Waite were outside, it was clear these guys all had machine guns.

"Get in the car," they said.

So they got in the car. They drove for maybe three blocks, and then piled into an elevator with these guys and their machine guns. The doors opened on the fourth floor, and there were two more guys with machine guns. They kept walking down the hall, past them.

"Now listen, when you go in here, keep your hands down at your side, don't reach into your coat for anything," they were explaining.

They went into the room, did not reach into their coats for anything, and sat down. A big guy came into the room and looked around.

"Who wants to meet the big guy?" he asked.

"I do," Babe said.

"I'm the big guy," he said.

It was Al Capone. Waite says he was scared to death. Babe, once he knew who he was, was happy to meet him. And Capone was happy to meet Babe. Hell yeah!

"Welcome to my town, boys," he said. "Have a good time."

To me Babe Ruth was the greatest player ever, hands down. I'm not even talking statistically, although if you crunch the numbers, they also tell you he was the greatest ever, not just a dominant, record-setting pitcher early in his career with the Red Sox, but the greatest power hitter ever, finishing with a lifetime batting average of .342, tenth-best of all time, to go with his 714 home runs, the most in history until Hank Aaron came along. He's the best ever in so many categories, including some of this new stuff—you know, WAR and OPS+ and all that.

To me Babe is the greatest ever because of the electric effect he had on people. Babe Ruth, because of his presence, would go into Detroit or Kansas City, or just some town he hit on a barnstorming tour, and for that weekend they would sell out every seat. Babe saved the game after the 1919 Black Sox scandal, when eight Chicago White Sox players were banned from baseball for losing the World Series on purpose, for money. I don't know of another player in any sport who could save his game the way Babe did. That's why he's the greatest player ever.

Three hundred years from now, people will talk about Babe Ruth. They won't talk about Barry Bonds, they won't talk about Hank Aaron, and they won't talk about Pete Rose. Babe was a true icon.

I'd also ask Waite about Ty Cobb, the all-time leader in hits. "If Ty Cobb was playing today, he would be the toughest son of a bitch in the league—and when I say tough, I'm talking about fighting," he told me during that 1963 season. "He was one mean son of a bitch, and he was big, like six-two, which was big for the 1920s. He was a hell of a ballplayer, but he was just nasty."

Cobb would stand out in the outfield, and if he bent down to pick up some grass, that was the signal that the Tigers' pitcher needed to knock the opposing batter on the ass straightway. And they did, every time, because on the Detroit Tigers, Ty was the man. Sixteen times one year, Ty Cobb gave one pitcher on his team the sign to plunk a batter, and he hit sixteen guys. The pitcher didn't have anything against any of these guys. Ty Cobb was running the goddamned team, and he didn't have to give a reason. That winter, Ty got this guy traded to Chicago, and Detroit and Chicago played the first week of the next season. Up steps Cobb against this pitcher who was his teammate the year before, and—wham!—he gets hit by a pitch.

"I hit sixteen for you last year, you son of a bitch," the pitcher said, walking in toward Cobb. "That one was for me!"

Ty Cobb didn't even take a shower after that game. He waited outside the dressing room for this guy to come out, and when he came out, Cobb went after him and started pounding his head into the cement. They had to have five people pull him off this guy. Cobb was going to kill him. That was how mean he was.

I learned early that you can't help your team if you've been kicked out of a game for fighting. We had fights break out during our games occasionally when I played, more so than now. Usually something happened, a dirty slide the week before when we were playing the same team, or someone knocked someone on their ass the inning before, and you retaliate, or you slide dirty into second, and a guy might react to that. Sometimes tempers flared, it was part of the heat of the moment, but it seemed like every time you had a big league fight, the wrong guy always seemed to get hurt. Someone would come in late to try to break it up and wind up with a broken finger or something. I wasn't a guy who started fights. If you start fights, you get tossed. You can't help the team if you're in the clubhouse listening to the game. You can't help the team if you're on the disabled list. Then again, you can't be afraid of a fight, or guys will pick up on that right away. You want them to have their doubts about what you'll do.

In August of my rookie year, *Philadelphia Daily News* columnist Larry Merchant wrote a column talking about how I had "the flame" and a bright future. "Pete Rose does not want to be like everybody else, and the chances are he won't be," Merchant wrote. "He'd like to be like someone who wasn't like everybody else either, Jackie Robinson. . . . Rose is six feet and 190 pounds, he has a high black crew cut, and he looks like he'll fight you. There are things he'd like to do in baseball. 'I'd like to be rookie of the year,' he said. 'I know I've got a chance if I keep going the way I am. I've scored 81 runs. I'd like to score 100.'"

By the time we wrapped up the season in St. Louis in late September, I had those hundred runs scored—101, to be precise. I went 3 for 6 my last day to coax my batting average up to .273. I had twenty-five doubles, nine triples, and six home runs. I saw it as a solid season, but more a starting point to build off of in the coming years. Baseball to me was about always finding a way to get better, to learn more, to make yourself stronger and smarter, to develop new skills and sharpen old ones.

I always worked hard because I enjoyed it. I enjoyed practicing.

When I took batting practice, I really worked hard because I figured people were out there watching me. I don't know when it came about, but eventually I told myself that you'd better play every game like it was your last, because it might be. You might get killed on the way home. And you want people to remember you in a positive way.

I'm a firm believer that when you're playing baseball, it doesn't matter what position you're playing—every time the ball is hit, everybody has to move. Everybody has to move because that fucking white rat will find you. If you're playing right field and the ball is hit to the third baseman, you'd better be backing up the first baseman. And if it's an overthrow there, then he's throwing to third, and the left fielder better be backing up the third baseman. Always go toward the ball, because it might end up in your hands.

A lot of times when a guy is stealing second base, the center fielder is standing out there picking his nose instead of coming forward so the runner can't take third if the ball gets by the second baseman.

It's just a matter of keeping your concentration on playing the game. Once you get in the habit of doing that, it's instinctive. I guarantee I made fewer mental errors than anybody. Physical errors are part of the game. Mental errors, like throwing to the wrong base or not running the ball out, are not part of the game, if you know how to play.

On October 30 that year I headed across the Ohio River for a three-hour drive to the army base at Fort Knox, Kentucky, to report for basic training and active duty. I guess I already had the buzz cut covered. Like my boyhood friend Eddie Brinkman, I chose the Army Reserves for my military service. He was in the next barracks over from me at Fort Knox. As a professional baseball player, you didn't want to take a chance and risk getting drafted, which would cost you two years of playing time. So you joined the reserves and went through basic training, then had two weeks of active duty every year for the next six years.

I was there at Fort Knox a few weeks later when we got the terrible news that President John F. Kennedy had been killed in Dallas, Texas. That was a sad, sad day—without a doubt my worst day at Fort Knox. The death of John Kennedy was so bad for our country. People were devastated, so you can imagine what the mood was like on a military base. It's different when you're serving in the military. The president is your commander in chief. You take that loss personally.

I remember on the base the flags were at half-mast, and we had to get to work preparing for a parade and ceremony honoring Jack Kennedy. Going through that experience there made me understand the significance of that national tragedy much better than if I'd never been there. Through most of my life up until then, I couldn't have cared less who the president was.

The next Tuesday, I pulled KP duty and had to start at 3 A.M. I was in there waxing the mess hall when someone came to tell me I had a phone call. It was Jack Lang, secretary of the Baseball Writers' Association of America.

"Congratulations, Pete," he said. "You are the National League Rookie of the Year."

My next call was to my dad to give him the news that eighteen of the twenty-one sportswriters casting votes went for me. I'd won easily.

Let's just say I wasn't that surprised.

"Rose worked for the rookie of the year title, freely talked about it and deserved it," Jim Selman wrote in the *Tampa Tribune*. "Rose was and is the brash, young rookie. He doesn't care, though, because he believes this bubbling, confident personality affects his ball playing. 'What the heck, I'm only human,' he said this summer. . . . 'What am I supposed to do, keep quiet just because I'm a rookie?'"

The Associated Press article credited me with becoming "a hallmark of aggressiveness" for the Reds that season, and mentioned that I was the first to win Rookie of the Year with the Reds since Frank Robinson in 1956. I thanked Frank and Vada for being there for me when no one else on the team was.

I didn't celebrate for long since I was still at Fort Knox with Company E, 11th Battalion, 3rd Training Brigade, which was no vacation. They take a lot of pride in making basic training an ordeal. Part of your training was to suit up with a ton of military equipment strapped to your back and then you were supposed to climb these three hills they have there, named—and I'm not making this up— Agony, Misery, and Heartbreak.

I took to military life. I did well enough that when basic training was over, they asked me to stay on longer at Fort Knox as a platoon guide to watch over the next group of grunts going through basic training. Everyone would be standing at attention out on the parade ground and it would be my job to keep them in line.

I was looking forward to another season with the Reds. I thought we were on the verge of winning it all, and I hoped some of the awkwardness of the previous year was a thing of the past. Second base was mine now, everyone knew. I was ready to start the new year off with a bang, choosing Saturday, January 25, for a big day in my life: my wedding. There was one small problem. That was also the day of the annual baseball writers' dinner where they wanted to personally present my award for Rookie of the Year.

How could I be in two places at once? Answer: by moving fast, and bringing my new wife, Karolyn, along with me. I'd met Karolyn when a friend introduced us at River Downs racetrack the previous July. She loved baseball, she was easygoing, and we had a lot of fun together, and I knew she'd be a great mother.

The wedding that morning was perfect. It was at St. William Catholic Church in Price Hill, and I even wore a tuxedo with a bow tie. Not easy to get me into one of those monkey suits! Karolyn wore a beautiful understated dress of silk and lace. The bad news was: no honeymoon! I had to get back to Fort Knox to finish out my active duty. We'd spend our first night as man and wife at a baseball writers' banquet. Well, not all of it. But even once we'd left there, I wanted to hang out some more with Art Shamsky and his wife. "He wanted my wife and I to stay up in the honeymoon suite with them!" Shamsky says now, still a little shocked after all these years. Art and his wife declined the invitation.

CHAPTER 13

Venezuela

I was a late bloomer. Like my dad before me, I was still growing in my early twenties, transforming physically. And it took time for my coordination to catch up with my body. I was as focused as an athlete could be on all aspects of competing at the highest level, from mental preparation to alertness to execution, and I was going to get everything I could out of my body. What I found, as I actually lived out being a star baseball player, was that I was able to continue to get better and better.

What is talent? We can debate it all day, right? Is talent superior hand-eye coordination that gives you some kind of hard-wired advantage with a task like hitting a tennis backhand or reacting to a high fastball? For an athlete, physical gifts are part of the package, no question. I couldn't have done the things I did on a football field as a teenager if my basic genetics, my DNA, were not pretty good when it came to athleticism. Stutter-stepping, using a little hesitation move to shuck a would-be tackler, cutting back and then cutting back again—that all took balance and quickness, and the video that exists of some of those runs is proof that I was a superior athlete. That's one kind of talent.

Drive is another kind of talent. Heart is another kind of talent. I'd even say hope is another kind of talent. I always believed in myself. I always believed in my future as an athlete. I always believed I'd somehow be getting better, taking on new challenges and mastering them. You have to want it, want it bad, but you also have to believe you can surprise yourself, amaze yourself. There was a famous quote about how the true definition of insanity was doing the same thing over and over again and expecting different results. Some people say that it was a quote from Albert Einstein, the smartest guy ever. Turns out he never said that. Which is good, because to me insanity is just the opposite: it's doing the same thing over and over *without* expecting different results.

I'd shown myself I belonged in the big leagues with my Rookie of the Year season in 1963. I went through a tough period earlier, when it looked like I might have lost my job to Don Blasingame, but I kept working at it, kept believing, and scored 100 runs, just like I wanted to. If you can score runs, you're helping your team win and that was always uppermost in my mind. We were a better team in '64 than we had been the year before, moving up from fifth place in the National League (86–76) to a second-place tie with Philadelphia, both of us at 92–70, one game behind the pennant-winning Cardinals.

We were better, but I'm not sure I was. I went into that year wanting to lift my average to .300, and instead it dropped a little, from .273 to .269. Instead of 101 runs scored, I had 64. My RBIs and doubles were down and, how about this, the king of the triple had only two three-baggers in 1964, down from nine the year before.

I'd laughed off the idea of any kind of sophomore slump after a strong rookie season, but I had trouble getting it going in 1964. My average wasn't all that far north of .200 in the early days. At the tail end of May, I was batting .215 after a 4-for-23 stretch. By June the papers were noting that I was "down in batting, though apparently in no immediate danger of losing [my] second base job."

In July, I went to see my uncle Buddy in Dayton. Uncle Buddy always did understand hitting, and specifically my swing, as well as anyone around. I was still scuffling along at .214, and he told me to "try holding the bat a bit lower and attack the ball." So that's what I did—and went on a 10-for-18 tear.

One thing bothering me that year was watching my manager Fred Hutchinson go through health issues. He and I had a good understanding, and when Dick Sisler took over, I got along with him, too, but it was a little different. Sisler would sit me down now and then when I was having troubles at the plate. That's what managers do, but I felt that with a Rookie of the Year award behind me, I deserved more patience.

August was a tough month for me, though. At one point I was stuck in a 2-for-28 slump and Sisler had me ride the pine again, starting in Houston, then on to San Francisco and Los Angeles. Chico Ruiz was playing at second instead of me, and Sisler was telling reporters he was trying to "jolt" me.

ROSE IS BENCHED AGAIN was the headline.

"The real difficulty—and I told him—is that he has not been hitting intelligently as a leadoff batter," Sisler told the *Enquirer*.

That stung, I'm not gonna lie. Sisler also claimed I'd refused an order, which wasn't true. It was all a misunderstanding. I was a second baseman and knew I was a second baseman, but Sisler had me come to his hotel room when the team was in LA and he chewed me out. So the next day, I strapped on catcher's gear for the first time in years and offered to catch batting practice. It was a weird time.

I was back in the starting lineup from September 10 on and got hot, batting at a .389 clip over the next nine games and helping me finish the season on a positive note. I knew I'd have some work to do in the off-season. The season came down to the last day. We lost to the Phillies, 10–0, and the Cardinals beat the Mets to win the pennant. That was a gloomy dressing room afterward. Fred Hutchinson, looking more frail all the time as he fought cancer, was sitting down in street clothes.

"I'm sorry that the team couldn't have won for that gentleman over there," Sisler said.

"I'm sorry that they couldn't have won for themselves," Hutch said.

Two weeks after the season, I flew down to Caracas, Venezuela, for my first experience of playing in a winter-ball league. I had to do that after the year I'd just had. I went there to hone my skills, not knowing what to expect, and found out it was a much better league than I could have imagined, with an electric atmosphere at the games and a lot of really good players. The reason I went with the Caracas Lions was I'd be playing for manager Reggie Otero, who was a coach with Cincinnati. I knew Reggie could help me improve my defense. You've got to watch it when you go to one of those countries in winter ball. If you're a pitcher, they'll pitch you till you can't wipe your ass. Reggie was just the right kind of guy for me to work with, because one, you know he's going to work you hard, and two, he's going to watch out for you and not abuse you.

I never minded working—and it turned out that was exactly what Reggie had in mind for me. Three teams played at the same stadium, so you had a lot of off days. One week we had one game, another week we had two games. At most you played three games in a week, so the league didn't wear you out. When we weren't playing, we were going to the park and practicing.

I knew I had to work on moving to my right to field grounders up the middle. Hutch always said he thought I was as good as any he'd seen going toward first base for a ground ball, but he never said that about me moving to my right. I knew it was my bat, not my glove, that had earned me the Rookie of the Year honor. I had to work out a lot of kinks, including turning double plays. Reggie helped me convert my throwing motion to more of a quick toss, instead of my natural long throwing motion.

"It is a game of departments," Reggie later told *Sports Illustrated*. "Throwing the ball is one department, catching it another. Each little thing is a department. The department here was the release of the ball. I had a coach hit ground balls and a kid at shortstop throw the ball to Rose. I would yell at him. It is a game of habit, you know. He had to get the habit. I didn't care where he had his feet, or whether he threw the ball fifty feet wild. When he learned to release the ball, we could work on that."

I don't know quite how it happened, but something definitely clicked for me down there in South America. I give Reggie Otero a lot of credit. I'd been working harder than everyone else for as many years as I'd been playing baseball, so sweating my ass off in the Caracas sun was just one more chapter of many. Maybe I'd grown enough and filled out enough and was strong enough that I could play the position differently than when I was a scrawny kid, or maybe something about Reggie's coaching style just suited me. I guess I'll never know for sure. But I know I liked the results.

"Baseball players are like ballerinas: They must practice until their feet are sore and then practice some more," Otero told *SI*. "In the tropical sun at high noon, releasing the ball for the 150th time, something besides their feet is likely to get sore. Oh, if Pete was a different kind of kid, he would have told me to go to hell. He would get so tired he'd fall down. I'd tell him to take five, and then we go some more."

I became popular in Venezuela. Every move I make on the field I make with passion, with intensity, with feeling, and the fans in Venezuela are passionate. They're smart and they're emotional and they know the game. Every game was sold out, and you felt like you were at some kind of festival, only it was a festival of baseball, a celebration of a great sport, a great spectacle, with fans who did not miss a thing. If you dived for a ball, they cheered. If you ran to first, they whooped. If you stretched a double into a triple with a headfirst slide into third base, kicking up a cloud of dust, they knew what you were up to practically the second you were out of the batter's box and then watched knowingly as you made your turn at first and busted it down toward second, sensing a triple the whole time.

If you made an error, they booed—well, no, what they did was whistle. If you made four errors in one inning—the way I did one time that winter—they whistled even more. I was half tempted to call it quits then and catch a plane back home, but I'm no quitter—and I knew if I didn't make some improvements, I might not be able to stay in the majors. I was so down after that game, I told Otero I'd had enough. He called me into his office.

"Look, if you don't stay down here and work your butt off, you're going back to Triple-A next year," he said, and I knew he was right.

I played the game the same way I did back at Boldface Park, the same way I played in Dayton Double-A and Geneva and Tampa and Macon. I played all out, just like I did every time I hustled my tail out onto a ball field anywhere in the world, from big league ballparks on both coasts to Osaka, Japan. I just played the game the way it's supposed to be played. Because of my enthusiasm, I won the hearts of the people in Venezuela.

But you know why else they loved me in Caracas? The fans in Venezuela would bet on everything that happened at the ballpark. They were constantly betting, but the big bet was on who would score the first *carrera*, the first run. I led off for the best team, hit .340, and led the league in runs scored, so they loved me, because I scored the first run more than anyone. They loved betting on me.

Every morning that we didn't have a game, before I went to practice, I'd go to the racetrack to watch them work out horses. Through one of my Venezuelan teammates, I met a jockey named Felix Garcia, and we became friends. He'd take me to this beautiful racetrack down in the valley in Caracas and we'd watch horses together and talk horses. I could talk horses all day, still can.

I was living with Tommy Helms again that winter. He was playing for Magallanes, another of the teams in the league, along with Valencia and La Guaira. We stayed at a hotel right across from the ballpark, and we had a place we liked to go for food where you sat outside in these gardens they had. It was local food and we'd get steaks and stuff, so we were happy.

I remember one night I was there having dinner with Tommy

and Ken Harrelson, my teammate on Caracas. We all called him Hawk Harrelson, because of that beak he had on him, and he was a great guy. He was playing for the Kansas City A's then, but he'd part ways with them in '67 when he denounced owner Charlie Finley as a "menace to baseball." Hawk always did speak his mind. He worked for years as a Chicago White Sox broadcaster and retired at the end of the 2018 season.

That night in Caracas, Hawk and Tommy got into an argument about which one of them could run faster. At first they were kind of joking, but they both got a little hot under the collar. These guys were crazy: Neither one of them was fast. They'd each had a few *cervezas* by this point. The next thing I knew, the two of them had decided to have a footrace right then and there to settle the issue. They pulled off their shoes to run barefoot, walked out onto the street and stopped traffic, then raced sixty-five yards. This was right off Bulevar de Sabana Grande in the center of town and people were everywhere. They were neck and neck right up until the end, and Tommy won in a photo finish. He had to beat Hawk, who was a lumbering first baseman. The only way Hawk could have won, given the size of his beak, would have been if he had bobbed his head at the last minute.

My team won the championship down there that year, the thirteenth winter in a row the Caracas Lions finished first in the league. I had good teammates. Hawk was our first baseman. Our third baseman was Damaso Blanco, who played later for the San Francisco Giants and then went back to Venezuela and did the announcing for the Caracas team. We also had Cesar Tovar, who grew up in Caracas shining shoes and played in Geneva the season before I did. Cesar would end up playing twenty-six seasons in the Venezuelan Winter

League, second only to another of our teammates that winter, Vic Davalillo. Those two were household names in Caracas.

I enjoyed Venezuela, but I was also glad that all four teams would be playing for two weeks in the Dominican Republic, where there were a lot of elite players as well. That year our visit to Santo Domingo was bittersweet. We were in a bus near downtown, and I was sitting next to Otero, who had the radio on. I didn't understand a word, but when his face dropped, I knew.

"Hutch?" I asked.

"He died," he said.

We were both pretty broken up after that. I'd miss Hutch, but I'd always hear his voice in my head, and I knew he'd have liked to see me work so hard that winter in Venezuela and forge myself into a better ballplayer than I had ever been. I'll be blunt: before that winter, I was not a big league second baseman. Sitting on my flight back home, I knew I could more than hold my own at my position—and I'd keep working, working, working to get better.

I hit .340 down there in Venezuela, and that got me off and running. After that I was a .300 big league hitter, no doubt. For the 1965 season, I batted .312, a nice improvement on my .269 average one year earlier, and that started a run of nine seasons in a row that I hit better than .300 in the major leagues. Before Venezuela I'd never had 200 hits in a season, but starting in '65 I had back-to-back 200-hit seasons, and I'd reach 200 hits in five of the next six seasons. So I turned a corner in Caracas and burned away some of my bad habits in the tropical heat.

CHAPTER 14

Hustling Little Pete Rose

A s late as May 1964, with more than a year in the big leagues under my belt, newspaper articles were still calling me Hustling Little Pete Rose. That had been my image for years, going back to school days, but by the 1965 season I was a grown man with a grown man's body. Guys by then were talking about bouncing off me. They were talking about me barreling into second base like a freight train when I went in hard to break up a double play. My weight had gone from barely 150 to up near 200 pounds, and I was strong.

That year I would go on to play in every single game the Reds played, all one hundred sixty-two games. I was no Lou Gehrig or Cal Ripken, but I had my own consecutive-games streak going. There were no more headlines about me being benched to give me a "jolt." I went from a rough sophomore season that inspired much talk of me being sent down to finishing sixth in the balloting for 1965 National League Most Valuable Player. Willie Mays was the MVP, with Sandy Koufax behind him for second place. To give you an idea of the company I was in, behind me (in order) were Hank Aaron, Roberto Clemente, Juan Marichal, Willie McCovey, and Joe Torre.

Late in June, the papers started guessing I'd be chosen as a starter for the All-Star Game that July, and they turned out to be right, with my fellow players voting me the starting second baseman. What an honor that was. That was my first All-Star Game, and I was nervous even before I arrived in Minnesota for the game and went into the locker room and saw that they'd put me right between Willie Mays and Hank Aaron, two-thirds of our starting outfield, along with Willie Stargell. Me, getting suited up right between Willie Mays and Hank Aaron? Then I was really nervous. I couldn't believe it. I slapped myself in the face and said, "What the hell am I doing here?"

Those were two of the greatest baseball players ever and they showed me nothing but respect. They treated me like I was one of the guys, like I was just another teammate trying to win the game, and I never forgot that. I always tried to do the same thing at the All-Star Game. I always went out of my way to make the young guys playing in their first All-Star Game feel good about themselves.

I always loved talking to Willie and Hank. They had the same traits as players, but they had very different personalities. Willie was really outgoing—The Say Hey Kid—and Hank was kind of quiet, but they both really liked to talk to young players about hitting.

I remember when I was a rookie in 1963 and we were out playing the Giants at Candlestick Park, the first concrete-bowl stadium in baseball, just three years after it opened. I was kidding Willie, who could turn and run after a ball hit over his head in center field like no one else.

"You better play me deeper," I told Willie.

He laughed at that.

"Man, you can't hit the ball over my head in this park," Willie told me.

So guess what? I got a pitch to hit and lined the ball right over his head for a double. Mays was still shaking his head in disbelief when he came in after the top of the inning and ran by me.

"I still don't believe it," Willie said. "You just ain't that strong."

Hank and I always talked about how we approached every pitcher. We were much different players. He was on his way to being the Home-Run King, and I'd wind up as the Hit King. I think he had an idea of what I went through to become the player I was. He appreciated how hard I worked. His teammate Ralph Garr had a style more like mine. I think Hank probably told Ralph, "You should play like this kid."

Roberto Clemente was another one who loved to talk hitting. At old Forbes Field, we had to walk underneath the stadium and then through the Pittsburgh dugout, to get to the visitors' dugout. Underneath the stadium were benches and Roberto would sit there and put on a clinic.

"Bobby, how are you feeling today?" I'd always ask him.

"Pete, let me tell you one thing, every bone in my body hurts," he'd say in that thick accent.

Then he'd go out and hit the ball all over the park, going 3 for 5. The next day, I'd ask him again and he'd say he felt great—then finish 0 for 4. That's why we always said we hoped he was feeling good.

Roberto Clemente helped me more than any player who wasn't my teammate. You had to listen closely to everything he was saying, because his English wasn't the greatest. So you paid more attention. Plus, he was Roberto Clemente, the greatest Puerto Rican ever to play the game. He was on that National League All-Star team as well, a reserve along with Frank Robinson, which is pretty amazing when you think about it.

There is only one way to become a master in your own right, and that's to learn as much as you can from masters. My dad, as I keep telling you, was a master of competition, and he taught me most of what I knew about hitting. To continue that education, I was able to get loads of advice from some of the greatest hitters ever: Mays, Aaron, Clemente, and countless others. It didn't matter if they were power hitters and my game was more singles and doubles. A lot of hitting is seeing, which starts with thinking, and those three guys were as good at that as anyone who ever played the game.

I was starting to feel like I was repaying my dad for all he'd given me and all he'd taught me. My winter in Venezuela was always with me, like a dream. I told reporters I wouldn't be an All-Star if not for all that work I'd put in with Otero. And sure enough, the day after the All-Star Game, which we won, the picture that ran in papers all over the country was of me leaping over Cleveland's Vic Davalillo, my teammate in Caracas, to complete an acrobatic double play.

I loved playing in the All-Star Game. The higher the energy in a game, the happier I was. I played as hard in an All-Star Game as I played every day. To me it was no exhibition. It was battle. I went hit-less, but did get on base via a walk—and yes, I ran down to first base.

REDS' ROSE IN FULL BLOOM was the headline on a feature that ran on me the next week in different papers, starting with the words "Since Pete Rose is a mixture of Pepper Martin, Enos Slaughter, and Leo Durocher, it's only logical that he would never do anything conventional." The writer thought it was funny that even though I'd made only twelve errors the year before at second, putting me in second place in the league for fielding average, I went to winter ball to work on my fielding. "It was like telling Mamie Van Doren she needed work on her figure," the writer concluded.

That October, when United Press International announced its major league all-star team, I was the overwhelming choice at second base, getting twenty votes from the panel of experts, compared with two for the Pirates' second baseman Bill Mazeroski, and one each for Bobby Richardson of the Yankees and Frank Bolling of the Milwaukee Braves. I'd batted .312 for the season with eleven home runs and eighty-one RBIs. I led the league in hits with 209.

That turned out to be the last year I got to play with the great Frank Robinson, one of the best friends I ever had in baseball. I was shocked when the news came in December 1965 that the Reds had traded him away. My favorite teammate was gone. We picked up Milt Pappas, one of the best starting pitchers in the game at the time, and reliever Jack Baldschun, a helpful addition to our bullpen, as well as Dick Simpson, but that was way too much to give up, and I was reeling when I heard the announcement.

"The Reds just traded the best ballplayer they ever had," I said that month.

It felt weird for me to think about taking the field in a Reds uniform without Frank as my teammate—that's how important he'd been to me. When I got to the big leagues, the best player on my team was Frank Robinson, so what did I do? I tried to be like him. I listened to everything he said. I patterned myself on him in some ways. Frank helped me understand that it was OK to play with fire in the big leagues. Tough luck if anyone didn't like it. We weren't there for popularity contests, we were there to win. If you wanted to slide headfirst into second base, then do it. If you wanted to run to first base, then do it.

Frank played hard every day. Teams would have meetings before they played us and tell the pitchers, "Don't throw inside to Frank Robinson! He'll get up and tear your head off!" He hung over the plate, but they wouldn't pitch him inside. He wasn't a fighter or a troublemaker, but he could go harder into second base than anyone I ever saw. He was a terror on the bases. He's one of the reasons why I was super aggressive on the bases.

We were a good team in '65 and won eighty-nine games, but finished fourth place in the National League behind the Dodgers, Giants, and Pirates. Help was on the way. We ended up having three National League Rookies of the Year in a span of six seasons—me in '63, then Tommy Helms in '66, and Johnny Bench in '68. Tommy had a cup of coffee with the Reds in '64, one at bat, and in '65 he was back in the big leagues long enough to hit .381 in limited action.

Finally, in 1966, he was in the big leagues to stay. TOMMY HELMS RAISING LOTS OF EYEBROWS NOW was the headline out of spring training. "When you talk about Tommy Helms, you've got to say he's a kid who came to beat you," said Dave Bristol, Tommy's manager in San Diego. "Tommy has good baseball instincts, good hands, gets the ball away quick, has good range, and you never find him sleeping in the field. He is strictly for the team."

It was great to be teammates again. Tommy and I always had a lot of fun together. I got to know his whole family. Tommy was born and raised in Charlotte, North Carolina, and when he and I played together in Macon and were roommates, there was a Sally League team in Charlotte, the Hornets, so we'd play games there. They were from Gastonia, which is right outside Charlotte. Larry, Tommy's brother, was a minor league ballplayer, and his mom and dad were great. Every time I went to Charlotte with the Helms family, it was like a damn party. They were a loud, wild bunch.

In those days, we used to meet the families of guys, especially if they were from towns that had baseball teams, because when we'd come to play the family would come to the ball game. I would go out to eat with them. I enjoyed it because it kind of reminded me of home.

You're not going to hear me going on about how tough it was to be traveling all the time as a baseball player. I never in my life used travel as an excuse for being tired or run-down. We had chartered flights, and a bus would drive right out onto the tarmac and pick us up right at the bottom of the plane. I used to lead the league in room service. I'd have room service when I got up in the morning, before I went to the ballpark. I'd eat in the room unless it was checkout day.

I made sure I never ate breakfast with Johnny Bench. I'll tell you why. When Johnny was eating, he didn't like it when people came up to him and asked for an autograph. He was on a hair trigger. I didn't like those kinds of interruptions either, but when they asked me, I signed. Johnny wouldn't do it, because if you start signing autographs, the next thing you know your eggs are cold. He could be rude when he was eating a meal, but what were you going to do? I went through a period where my favorite meal was a chef's salad, because if I didn't order a chef's salad, my food was going to be cold by the time I got to it, I was signing so many autographs.

When the Reds went to St. Louis to play the Cardinals, I got to know Art Shamsky's family. I met his dad, Bill, and his mom, Sadie, and his Uncle Max, who was a great baseball fan. Art was born in University City, a suburb of St. Louis, and came from a nice Jewish family. There weren't a lot of Jewish ballplayers back when I played. Artie was a smart guy. He had a girlfriend from St. Louis named Randy who he ended up marrying.

Dave Bristol was always one of my favorites in baseball. I loved playing for him; he always made me laugh. I was happy when he became Reds manager again midway through the 1966 season. The guys would play for Dave, I was sure. And I knew he believed in me. He understood what made me tick in a way not every manager did.

He always liked to talk about his first impressions of me going back to when he managed me in Macon. "He didn't hit a ball, he attacked it," he said at one point. "He was like a guy breaking up a dogfight. He loved to hit and hit and hit. You go to his hotel room at night and he's hitting the bed post."

Some of the best advice I ever got was in that letter Reds scout Slugger Blomski sent me when I was in Geneva, New York, playing D ball. He helped me see things from the organization side and think like them when I could, like on changing position. Your goal as a ballplayer is to be in the lineup doing all you can to help the team win. If they feel you can do that best learning a new position, then let's get down to doing the extra work to make the adjustment and get up to speed.

So when Dave Bristol started sounding me out in spring 1967 about whether I might be ready to move to left field, I remembered that advice. I'd worked hard to get good at second base! I didn't want to learn a new position. But if Dave Bristol believed it was one more way for me to help the team, then I was game.

"Pete Rose is ready to tackle the outfield with a genuine conviction he'll eventually field the position well," wrote the Dayton paper that spring. "Bristol has made it plain to Pete that he doesn't expect him to turn into a Frank Robinson overnight."

It wasn't that bad learning to play left field. I could catch fly balls, and being a second baseman helped me as an outfielder, because having been the cutoff man, I'd know just where to expect the cutoff man to turn up. Learning one new position helps you learn another new position.

Going into the '67 season, I had four seasons with the Reds behind me, and let's just say I was a long ways from the excited kid who felt like pinching himself when he scored the first run of the '63 season on a Frank Robinson home run. Hey, I still feel like pinching myself, just replaying moments like that in my mind. But I had enough experience by then to know my way around, and I'd been through some disappointments.

Dave Bristol had known me and a lot of the other guys for a long time, and as the youngest manager in baseball he understood us better than some managers might have. "These are the guys I was raised with," he said in May 1967. "I knew them from way back. I don't baby them. I don't mollycoddle them. I let them know the ground rules and we go on from there."

I batted .359 that May and had a twenty-five-game hitting streak that ended in early June, when I was only two games behind Vada Pinson's team record. People got a kick out of the fact that I always knew what my batting average was during the season. The reason I knew was because in those days, the papers ran the top ten players in batting average every day and I was always there. Most guys had to wait until Sunday, when the papers published the batting average for every player in baseball. Somebody would ask what I was hitting, and I'd tell them.

"How did you know that?" they might ask.

"I just read it in the paper this morning."

I was doing fine in left field, but learning a new position always challenges you in new ways. You think you're doing good, and then something happens. That June, we were in LA and I had to make a diving catch on Willie Davis's sinking line drive to shallow left-center. I really had to haul ass to get to that ball, and stretched out making the grab, then rolled onto my shoulder. I felt something right away.

I hated missing games and I hated coming out of games, and even with my shoulder barking at me, I wasn't going to take myself out of the game. Play through the pain, that was always the thing. Ron Fairly came up and singled to left and I fielded a ball and made a strong throw home to try to get Wes Parker, but that was when I knew I was done. They sent me in for X-rays, which showed I had some kind of deep bruise where the collarbone meets the shoulder. I wanted to avoid going on the disabled list if I could, and the team was with me. In the end I missed eleven games, and the worst part was, Dave Bristol barred me from sitting in the dugout during games.

"I was afraid I'd be tempted to use him," Dave told reporters. "He'd come down and play pepper and warm up in practice, but it just wasn't worth taking the chance. I wasn't going to risk him and I didn't want to be tempted. He's too valuable."

Even when I was back in the lineup, my shoulder still hurt, but at least I didn't miss the three weeks you lose when you go on the twenty-one-day DL. In my whole career, I was only on the DL two times.

I was healthy in time for the 1967 All-Star Game, and manager Walter Alston chose me as one of the reserves. The papers noted that I would be a "versatile" addition to the team, mentioning that I could "play any infield posts and the outfield if needed" but did not add that I could even catch, in a pinch, since that was my position for so many years coming up.

Dave Bristol was a young manager, but he didn't lead like a young manager, he led like a guy who'd been writing out big league lineup cards for years and years. The job of the manager is above all to understand each and every one of his players and to know how to reach them. My manager later on, the great Sparky Anderson, liked to talk about how there are three—and only three—ways to reach a guy: You kick him in the ass, you leave him alone, or you give him a pat on the back. The trick was knowing which kind of guy a given player was. That same month, July 1967, we were in a funk at the plate as a team, and Dave decided it was time to impose a fine on anyone who came up with a runner on third base and no outs or one out, and did not bring that runner home.

Guess who earned the first fine from the new rule? Yours truly, that's who. I had four hits, including three extra-base hits, and we cruised to a 6–2 win over the Pirates, but in the seventh I came up with runners on the corners and one out, and bounced out. After the game, I walked right in to see Dave in his office and handed him twenty-five bucks in cash and a trading stamp catalog I'd won for being on a radio show. Dave said he wanted the full fifty bucks and wouldn't accept the catalog.

"Maybe he needs it for his wardrobe," I told reporters that night. But I made clear I thought it was a good rule, and I was happy to pay the fine. I was on an 11-for-19 tear and had my average back up to .331.

I flew out to Anaheim for my second All-Star Game and even though I wasn't starting, I felt honored to be there with so many great players. Our pitching staff alone was amazing. Juan Marichal started the game for the National League and threw three shutout innings, then Fergie Jenkins gave up one run in his three innings—and Bob Gibson, up next, also shut out the AL. For the AL it was a pitching tag team of Dean Chance, Jim McGlothlin, and Gary Peters that worked the first eight innings, also allowing one run, so we were all tied up going into the ninth, and it went into extra innings.

I almost didn't get into that game! I was sitting on the bench until the fourteenth inning, when Alston sent me out to play second base. I'd made the team as an outfielder and was going in as a second base-man, but the reason Alston held me out of the game as long as he did was that I was the only one he had left who could catch, if necessary. That's a fact. So finally I got a chance to pinch hit in the fourteenth and went out and played defense and made a good play, and then we won it in the fifteenth on a Tony Perez home run.

I was still making headlines in 1967 just for playing the way I played. In late August, there was one article, PETE ROSE: HE TAKES DULLNESS OUT OF WALKING, that quoted Bob Hoswam, the Reds' general manager, talking about my running to first base even on a walk. "He has taken what many fans consider the dullest play in baseball and made it into one of the most exciting," Bob said. "There seems to be an electrifying surge throughout the ballpark as Pete takes off for first, and the fans really enjoy it."

We'd been in first place in the National League for a total of forty-nine days early in the season, but injury after injury knocked us out of contention. We fell out of first on June 16 and never bounced back. It was just one of those years. I'd hit .300 for the third straight season after my winter league experience in Caracas, but no one else on that team hit .300. Guys had off years, and we just didn't generate enough offense. I fell short of two hundred hits after two seasons of making it.

If the Reds had not won anything in the years to come, you could look back at the Reds teams of those years and see a club that looked out of the mix. But we knew better. We knew we were putting together the talent and that it was being developed the right way. Dave Bristol had taken over midway through the '66 season, so '67 was his first full season as Reds skipper, and he was starting to put his stamp on the team. He would only have three full seasons before the Reds hired Sparky Anderson, who I loved as well, but Dave made his mark. I always tell people looking back on the Big Red Machine teams I played on that, as much credit as Sparky gets for developing those great Reds teams, Dave put that team together. He managed so many of the guys in the minor leagues and instilled in us good baseball values and good baseball sense. He taught me so much about winning and about taking care of myself over the long season.

CHAPTER 15

Vietnam

Late in the 1967 season, I got a call from someone who worked at
the State Department.

"Would you be interested in going to Vietnam?" he asked me.

My first thought was: *I already done my service in the Army, so no
one's drafting me to go fight in the jungle.* I was twenty-six then. But I
didn't say nothing. I was curious what this fella from the State Department might want with me.

"I don't know," I told the man. "There's a war going on over
there."

I wasn't one to pay much attention to the news. I didn't sit down
and watch old Walter Cronkite on the TV or anything like that. But
even if you were ignoring the war, you heard about it all the time and
had a pretty good idea there were half a million young Americans
fighting in Southeast Asia. Just what they were doing over there no
one seemed to know, something about helping South Vietnam try to
fight off communists from North Vietnam. What we did know was

that a lot of them were coming home in body bags. Why in hell would I want to fly halfway around the globe to get closer to that war?

"Well," the State Department man said, "Joe DiMaggio's going."

"I get to meet Joe?" I asked, and my voice might have cracked a little, I was so excited at the idea.

"Meet him?" the man said. "You'd get to live with him. You'd be over there for more than two weeks."

I'd never met Joe DiMaggio. He was retired from the New York Yankees long before I came up, so our paths had never crossed. All I knew about Joe were two things: he had been married to Marilyn Monroe, making him the envy of about every man on the planet, and he hit in fifty-six straight games. Another thing I knew about Joe was he drank coffee—I guess that's a third thing I knew. We all saw him in those ads for Mr. Coffee that seemed to be everywhere in those years.

I was going to fly all the way over to Vietnam to get to know Joe, one of the greatest ballplayers that ever lived! He was a great athlete, fun to watch, always consistent. He finished with 361 home runs in his career and had only 369 career strikeouts. In 1967, Joe was an executive vice president of the Oakland A's—that was sixteen years after his last season with the Yankees in 1951—but he was still Joe DiMaggio.

I wasn't sure how I felt about dropping into the middle of a war. I didn't really like the idea of anyone shooting at me or launching mortars in my direction. We'd be traveling around South Vietnam trying to boost morale, and they'd even told me they'd suit me up in a colonel's uniform. The idea was, if we were captured, we'd be treated as officers and not as spies.

The whole thing was set up by the USO, which used to bring Bob Hope over to entertain the troops, usually with a chesty blonde on his arm, sometimes a Playboy playmate. Times had changed. Bob put on shows for the troops. For us it would be different. We'd be heading into the thick of the action.

I'm not gonna lie, I was scared.

We all gathered in San Francisco at the end of October 1967. Tony Conigliaro of the Red Sox was the only other active ballplayer coming on the trip. Tony flew out to San Francisco, along with Yankees broadcaster Jerry Coleman and Bob Fishel, the PR director for the Yankees. Joe and I met up with them in San Francisco on Halloween night, and we all went down to Fisherman's Wharf and had dinner at DiMaggio's restaurant. I was on cloud nine just having dinner with Joe, and I was on cloud nine the whole trip, finally getting a chance to hang out with the great DiMaggio.

Our flight from San Francisco to Tokyo felt like it took about a week. There was no first class or anything like that, and Joe and I sat up in the first row, so at least we could put out our feet and stretch our legs a little. I wasn't used to being in the air so long for an international flight. I'm still not used to that—I never will be. I remember we had to land in Guam to gas up. At least we got a short break from being cooped up in that plane for twenty hours.

From Tokyo they flew us down to Saigon, the capital of South Vietnam, and our first stop was to a field hospital there. That hit us hard. Everywhere you went, you saw guys who had their legs blown off or lost an arm. That war was all booby traps and grenades. It tore me up seeing guys more or less my age sacrificing so much to serve our country. To this day I have the utmost respect for anyone who served in the military. I always make a little extra time to talk to them and honor their service.

We'd walk around, and these GIs couldn't believe what they were seeing. Joe DiMaggio himself! They were handing out flyers of our "Major League Roundup," with "USO" at the top in big, sparkling, red-white-and-blue lettering, and a picture of Joe in pinstripes: "The Yankee Clipper." They put me right at his side, a kid ballplayer just filling out his big league uniform, and that's where I was for all seventeen days of that trip, at Joe's side whenever I could be.

I remember one day on that trip when we were in helicopters landing at a base and tracer fire arced up out of the jungle toward some of the choppers in front. Joe and I were riding in a helicopter in the back and I remember thinking, *If this chopper goes down and we're all killed, nobody's gonna even know I was on board. Every story's gonna be about Joe DiMaggio. Who in the hell's gonna care about Pete Rose?*

Joe was modest and relaxed the whole time. Well, almost the whole time. I do remember him getting mad during one of our hospital visits those first two days in Saigon. We knew the Viet Cong had their own hospital and were told they had air-conditioning there. So we went to a hospital to visit our soldiers and it was so hot and stuffy, we couldn't believe it. You felt like you were suffocating, just standing there. Joe got really pissed off about that.

"How in the hell do they have air-conditioning over at the VC hospital, and our guys don't have air-conditioning?" he yelled.

We stopped by to see one guy who'd taken a direct hit from a mortar, and he had open wounds all over the place. Attendants would stop by every half hour to turn him over.

"Man, I can't wait to get out of here, so I can get them bastards," he told Joe and me. "I can't wait to get out of this war so I can go and get the sumbitch who did this to me."

That guy had some *cajones*. We saw that everywhere we went, young guys a long way from home showing amazing courage. Back home, there were polls that said almost as many people had come to feel the Vietnam War was a mistake as supported it, and that same month we were there, Secretary of Defense Robert McNamara, who oversaw the war effort, announced he was resigning. We didn't talk politics with the soldiers or officers we met, we just did our best to show our support and thank them for their service.

As much as I was in awe of Joe DiMaggio, I was even more in awe of William Westmoreland, the four-star general who was in charge of all the US forces in Vietnam. If I could have been anything, I'd like to have been a general. We met Westmoreland in Saigon right at the start of that trip, and I couldn't believe I was talking to him. Well, not that I was doing much talking. He was just talking to Joe, more or less. I was along for the ride. I was just a kid, no matter how I'd been playing on the field, and I knew when I should pipe down and fade into the background.

Everywhere the generals went in Vietnam, they had to have air-conditioning in the cars, because if they had the windows down, someone might run up and try to throw a grenade into the open window. Soon after he met with us, Westmoreland was summoned back to Washington by President Lyndon B. Johnson, and told reporters as soon as he arrived at Andrews Air Force Base that he was "very, very encouraged" by the progress in the war. On that trip he predicted that US troops would start going home from Vietnam "within two years or less." We could understand his optimism. That was how it seemed to us, too, meeting with all those soldiers.

After two days in Saigon, our USO group split up. Jerry Coleman and Tony Conigliaro headed north and Joe and I went with Bob Fishel, the Yankees PR exec, down where the Mekong River flows into the South China Sea.

I was so glad they had me in the same group as Joe. We'd hear mortars going off all around us, and rockets being fired out of helicopters, and I was so scared I didn't even know how scared to be. But Joe never flinched. Once I saw Joe's demeanor, how he treated the situation and how he treated the soldiers, my fear went away and I was actually happy. My philosophy was: If it's good enough for Joe DiMaggio, it's good enough for me. He was so polite, so humble, everywhere we went.

There we were, down in remote parts of South Vietnam where these soldiers wouldn't see an American from back home for months. They're down in the Mekong Delta, teaching these Vietnamese how to fight, and all of a sudden in walks Joe DiMaggio, the Yankee Clipper. They couldn't believe it! I just stood in the back and shook my head in amazement. He was so down-to-earth, he didn't even mind my kidding him.

"Hey, World's Greatest Player, let's get going," I'd say to Joe.

It was hot in Saigon and even hotter down there where we were with the troops.

"I've got to take a shower," Joe said to me one day.

A shower? Out here?

"Joe, we're not in downtown Saigon," I said.

He didn't care. He wanted to take a shower. The only way you could do it out there in the jungle was for one guy to stand up on a chair and feed water into a big canvas bag, and you pulled a lever and the guy underneath got a shower. So that's what I did so Joe could have his shower. I've got to be the only guy in the world to give Joe DiMaggio a shower. I had a good look at him and I'll just say this: Yankee Clipper my ass. Joe DiMaggio was a penis with a man hanging from him. I felt sorry for Marilyn Monroe.

I remember one time climbing up into one of those Huey helicopters and being taken for a ride. A captain was flying the helicopter that day and next to him was a brigadier general. Joe and I were in the back, and right next to each of us was a door gunner whose job it was to operate an M60 machine gun and try not to get shot himself. The story that went around Vietnam was that the average life span of a Huey door gunner was five minutes.

We lifted off, the big rotor cutting the air like a hurricane, to where dust and grit was flying every which way, and that pilot pushed his stick forward and we shot out of there. We were flying along like a bat out of hell. One of the door gunners told me we were flying at 130 knots, which works out to 150 miles per hour, and we were just clearing the trees. I kept sneaking looks up ahead to make sure we weren't about to run into a branch. Joe had that big, easy smile, like he'd seen it all before.

"That brigadier told them to take us on a joy ride," he told me, laughing.

We were in the heart of the Mekong River Delta, down near Saigon at the lower tip of Vietnam. I kept a good grip and watched the door gunners, figuring if they were calm, I could be calm, too. Finally we landed and Joe went over to talk to the brigadier, smiling.

"That was a good joy ride," he told the general.

The general was not smiling.

"Joe," he explained, "we have to fly at treetop level or they'll shoot you out of the sky with a rocket."

We hadn't thought of that. The brigadier was just trying to keep us all alive.

It takes you a while to get your legs back after a helicopter ride like that. We were in a town called Cai Nhum, and it turned out the Viet Cong had tried to overrun the village the night before.

A colonel took us for a walk around town, and in the middle of the street we saw five bodies wrapped up in bamboo with their feet sticking out. I'm just a damn naive kid, twenty-six years old, and I kind of tapped my foot up against the foot of one of those corpses. I don't know why I did it, I just kind of did it. I'd never seen anybody dead before.

"Don't do that," the colonel said.

"I'm sorry, sir," I said. "Why not?"

"The Viet Cong always come back for their dead," he told me. "All five of those bodies are booby-trapped."

Our troops had wired the bodies with explosives, hoping the Viet Cong would come back for them and be blown sky-high. There I was, sticking my foot out, a rambunctious kid seeing things I'd never seen before. Smoke was heavy in the air, and walking around town, you could still hear mortar fire pounding in the background. I counted nineteen body bags, meaning nineteen dead marines.

"You see that and you know a war is going on," I told reporters at the time.

The navy picked us up and flew us out to an aircraft carrier patrolling the South China Sea. It was an old Essex-class carrier, the USS *Intrepid*. Name sound familiar? The *Intrepid* would later end up docked along the Hudson River in Manhattan. Just landing on that big ol' bathtub was an adventure. It's cruising along at thirty knots, and when your plane lands, it has a big hook that has to catch on a cable running across the flight deck. I was kind of sweating it out, but I looked over at Joe and he was calm as can be, so why wouldn't I be calm, too?

We got catapulted off that aircraft carrier when it was time to leave. That was kind of scary, too. You take off and then the plane dips way down. You don't know if you're going to go in the drink or not, and if you do go in the drink, the ship's going to run over you, because it's going so fast.

They had us sit in on a pilots' meeting as they were getting their flight plans and instructions for a bombing run on Hanoi, the capital of North Vietnam, where the Vietnamese revolutionary Ho Chi Minh was still living then. We went out on the deck afterward and Joe took a piece of chalk, went up to one of the bombs on the plane and scrawled a message out.

"Fuck Ho!"

The pilot loved that. He came up to Joe after that bombing run with a grin on his face.

"I got an ammunition dump with that bomb," he told him.

Joe was proud. He'd served two and a half years in the US Army during World War II, and he still thought like a soldier.

That was the trip of a lifetime for a kid from Cincinnati who hadn't hardly been out of the country: flying all the way around the globe and hanging out with Joe DiMaggio and having bullets whizzing around and talking to wounded soldiers and meeting generals.

That was the closest I ever got to fighting in a war. (Waxing floors at Fort Knox doesn't count.) I don't know about war. None of it made any sense to me at all.

CHAPTER 16

Batting Title

I f you were a ballplayer back in my era, you played for peanuts, but no one ever wanted to hear you talk about money. Owners could make money, and the TV networks that showed the games could make money, but players were expected to act happy just to be paid at all for playing a game for a living. The truth was, I'd have played baseball for nothing, I loved everything about it so much, but I was a professional, with a professional's responsibilities, and going into the 1968 season I had three straight .300 seasons under my belt and expected a decent raise.

That January, I was a runner-up for the Hutch Award, named for the man who had more to do with me moving up the ladder in the Reds' farm system than anyone, Fred Hutchinson. The award was given to a player who showed "character and fighting spirit," and I was happy to have been voted one of the runners-up to Carl Yastrzemski, behind Bob Gibson and ahead of Tim McCarver.

I asked for $60,000 that year, the same amount Vada Pinson wanted, and he and I were two of eight Reds players who decided to hold out that spring and not report to spring training until we'd gotten a decent bump in pay. Just for comparison's sake, if you adjust for inflation, $60,000 back then would work out to about $435,000 in 2019 dollars. Now keep in mind, the Major League minimum salary for 2019 is $515,000, meaning the absolute minimum any player can earn, including the rawest rookie or a journeyman utility infielder.

Yet at the time, we were made out as gold diggers if we wanted a share in the profits. Here's how *New York Times* baseball writer Joseph Durso put it in a March 1968 article from spring training headlined BASEBALL GOLD RUSH IS LURING PLAYERS AND CLUB OWNERS: "Palm trees aren't the only things rustling in Florida this spring," Durso wrote. "The baseball natives are growing restless, too. The owners want new territories, the managers new rules, and the players new money. What everybody wants is 'the gold in them hills.'"

The minimum salary in baseball had just been raised from $7,000 to $10,000 ($72,000 in 2019 dollars).

The *Cincinnati Enquirer* visited me at home in early March and had some fun with their article.

"Flashy Pete Rose, attired in the mod-look of white turtleneck shirt, which blended perfectly with the jazz music on the hi-fi, leaned back in a plush couch in his apartment and quipped: 'Don't quite know when I'll begin writing my column,'" wrote reporter Bill Anzer.

"As had been announced, Pete was to be a guest columnist for the *Enquirer* during spring training. Friday, however, he was nowhere near a typewriter or a ball field, concentrating instead on some 'twisting' with his three-year-old daughter, Fawn. Before the brush-haired Rose can launch his career as a journalist, he has to iron out his contract wrinkles."

I was getting antsy and the Reds knew it. I was born to be outside, born to be mixing it up on a baseball field, and sitting at home playing with my daughter was great for a while—until it wasn't. Phil Seghi of the Reds and I had talked so many times, we were finishing each other's sentences. He was friends with Uncle Buddy, and he and I always got along great. Finally, when he called me at home on March 5, I agreed to a salary of about $55,000 and caught a plane for Florida a few hours later. I'd also missed a couple weeks that spring fulfilling my active-duty obligation to the army, so I wanted to get as many swings in as I could to help me callous up my hands and get ready for the season.

I'd always told myself to follow the advice given to me years earlier by Reds scout Slugger Blomski. The Reds had moved me from second base to left field, and now I was moving to right field, which was fine with me. But I needed games out there, and that spring training I'd get in barely two weeks since I had missed so much time.

One of the worst days of my life on a baseball field was an exhibition at the end of that spring training. We flew to Birmingham, Alabama, to play against the Oakland A's. On April 4, the night before the game, word reached us that the Reverend Martin Luther King Jr. had been assassinated. Now keep in mind, I wasn't what you'd call real politically aware, but I knew what a tragedy this was for my friends on the field and I knew what a tragedy it was for America.

The assassination came at a time when it already felt like things were spinning out of control in this country. Not long after I toured Vietnam with Joe DiMaggio, the North Vietnamese launched the Tet Offensive, the largest attack of the year. Some of the places Joe and I visited were right in the middle of the fighting. The week before Dr. King was killed, President Johnson went on TV and shocked everyone by making the announcement that with the country so divided over the Vietnam War, he would not seek reelection. "There is division in the American house now," Johnson said. "There is divisiveness among us all tonight."

The day after King was assassinated, Charles O. Finley, the A's owner, one of the real characters in the game, was there in Birmingham and did a press conference where he announced that Joe DiMaggio would not only be a vice president for the A's, he was also going to be in uniform as an A's coach. It was great to see Joe again. After telling him in Vietnam about what a good player I was, I couldn't wait to go play, knowing he was there, watching. But it was hard to keep my mind on baseball on a day like that.

That might have been the worst I ever played in my whole life. I always say that never in my baseball career did I throw to the wrong base and that's true—except that game. I made two errors: I dropped a fly ball and I threw to the wrong base. I also struck out three times. Joe was seeing me play for the first time and I stunk up the joint. I can't tell you how much that ate me up.

I had more military service that weekend, and then we were scheduled to open our season at home. Those plans were changed. Riots broke out in cities all over the country, including Cincinnati, where they imposed a curfew. President Johnson declared April 7 a national day of mourning for Dr. King, and he was memorialized with two funeral services on April 9. We wouldn't open our season until April 10, so I had several extra days to get ready—which I needed in the worst way. I went to the ballpark Sunday and took batting practice. I hit and hit and hit. Then I went back to the ballpark on Monday and did the same thing again. I was sore, but I knew I had work to do. On Tuesday I went back to the ballpark one more time and hit some more.

By Wednesday I felt ready, and I could start to get excited about the start of another season. For years we'd had the feeling as an organization that something was building. There was so much talent in the farm system, and the Reds' coaches in those years taught the game right. They helped young players develop solid fundamentals and a good understanding of the game so that by the time they hit the big leagues, they were quality players. We had our 1966 Rookie of the Year, Tommy Helms, and we had Tony "Big Dog" Perez, my friend since Geneva, who had broken through the year before with his first All-Star season, hitting .290 with 26 homers and 102 RBIs.

We also had a young catcher, Johnny Bench, who'd joined us late the year before. I'd read about him in the minor leagues and knew it was just a matter of time. We all knew that when he got there, he was going to be there a long time because he was so talented. He could do everything but run, and he didn't need to run. Even then it was obvious he was as strong defensively as any catcher you'll ever see, and I was sure he was going to hit. So was Ted Williams, who saw him hit that year and predicted (correctly) that he'd be a Hall of Famer one day.

Johnny had a great arm and all the physical tools, and he was also a smart game caller, knowing what guys could hit and what they couldn't hit. He called his own game and never looked over to the dugout, not like guys now. He was a take-charge guy who would sometimes get frustrated with pitchers if they shook off his signs. He had a knack for calming pitchers down when they were a little jumpy, but he also knew how to light a fire under a guy.

As *The New York Times* explained in one story about Bench, dating to the late '60s, he was catching relief pitcher Gerry Arrigo, who was getting very little on his fastballs. Bench kept trotting out to the mound to urge him to throw a little harder. No dice. "He went out one more time and gave him the word, then went back to the plate, settled into his crouch, and grimly called for a fastball," the *Times* reported. "Arrigo went into the big windup and fired the ball chest-high and a little outside, without much speed. Bench barely moved to catch the pitch. He just casually stuck up his bare hand, caught the ball and snapped it back to the pitcher harder than it had come to the plate—all without moving out of the crouch."

I can tell you this: Some pitchers didn't like to throw to Johnny. They were intimidated and didn't want to shake him off. Sometimes a pitcher might think he had a guy set up for a curveball and then Johnny would call for a fastball, but in my experience Johnny was usually right. He's the best of all time. You can't get any better than that.

I had only one hit on Opening Day against the Cubs, but by the fifth game of the season, against the Cubs at Wrigley, I had a 4-for-5 game and felt like I was getting going. By late April I was hitting .400, having gone 20 for 50 to that point with six doubles and a couple of home runs.

I'd settled for less than sixty grand in salary so I could go to spring training, but I knew I was worth more, the way I brought fans out to the ballpark. By 1968, I'd started to get a little fixated on the idea of making six figures a year. That was the kind of money home-run hitters made. I was more of a singles hitter, though I was always look-ing for the extra-base hit and even poked my share of homers.

"Why am I so set on getting $100,000?" I told reporters. "It's a figure athletes like to shoot for. Not everybody can say, 'I'm making $100,000.' Guys like Willie Mays, Hank Aaron, Roberto Clemente, and Mickey Mantle can say it, but they're all long-ball hitters. I'm not."

The way I saw it, I was already committed to doing everything I could to keep getting better, and if all that work paid off and showed some results, that would make my argument easier next time I was in contract talks.

Some of the other guys resented me for all the publicity I seemed to get every step of the way. I'm not talking about the stars, all those great players I had as teammates and friends, but maybe some of the other guys who wouldn't have minded seeing their name in print a little more. I made for a good story when I was first making it in baseball, a little runt kid from Cincinnati who made Rookie of the Year for the Reds, and my whole style of play might have rubbed some people the wrong way, but it made for good copy.

I knew that writers enjoyed writing about me, and I found that if I relaxed and enjoyed myself talking with them, usually they came away happy. I'd tell any young ballplayer the same thing now: Writers don't need much, they just need you to open up enough to give them a little glimpse of what it's like to be you, of how you saw a game, of how you see your teammates, almost anything. When Barry Bonds was at the top of the baseball world, just an amazing athlete, ESPN had a reporter following him full time. Bonds hated it and did his best to give that reporter nothing. If I knew how, we'd have invented reality TV before there ever was reality TV, and I'd have come up with a few minutes of decent stuff every day. The point is: It's not that hard. Just be yourself. What have you got to lose?

I had a story to tell, which was about a kid who didn't have the most talent or the best body for sports, but who was going to get everything he could out of his talent, a kid who played as hard as he could every day, every minute, and stayed as focused and mentally sharp as he possibly could, looking for ways to beat you. I think that was something sportswriters could relate to since a lot of them felt like it was hard work rather than talent that got them wherever they were. Some of the articles about me laid it on pretty thick, even I had to agree. What could I say? You take the good with the bad.

PETE ROSE MAKES BASEBALL LIVE was the headline on a column by Milton Richman of United Press International that ran in a lot of papers in May 1968. I was off to a good start that season, call it a great start, leading baseball with a .366 average, and that was the season known as the Year of the Pitcher. I was practically the only guy doing well at the plate.

"Pete Rose is the last of the red hot spenders," Richman wrote. "The way he spends his time and energy is a pure delight to behold. . . . Baseball never could be called a dying game if they all played it the way Pete Rose does."

I explained to Milton: "I wouldn't run if I didn't want to. I run after I get a base on balls because the catcher may miss the ball. I make a big turn at first base because I'm not satisfied with first. Too many guys are satisfied. Not me."

He asked me who hustled the most in the big leagues and of course I told him, "Me!"

"Pete Rose wasn't bragging," Milton wrote. "He was simply stating a fact."

A better way to put it was that I was always working harder than everyone else. It was just my nature. I didn't do it to make an impression, I did it to get results. If I wasn't making myself better, I felt like I was losing, and I hated losing. I was very thorough in my preparations. For years I'd been taking extra swings, and I still did that.

I never admitted when I was in a slump. Why do that? If you admit you're in a slump, then they've got you. If I felt like I was in a funk—or even if I'd had three hits in a game but something didn't feel right—I would take extra batting practice in the cage underneath the stadium right after the game, when I was still lathered up and still thinking about what I did right or wrong. I didn't wait until the next day. That was the time to work on something, just after the game, when it was still fresh in your mind what you were doing.

I might have played more pepper than any man in history. I don't know if today's big leaguers even play pepper. You see NO PEPPER signs at the ballpark, which is about the most ridiculous thing I ever saw. I played pepper every day with two or three batboys for about half an hour before batting practice. They'd toss the ball to me, just a soft toss, and I'd choke up a little and take a quick, light swing, just punching the ball back, then one of them would field and toss the ball again, and I'd hit it back the same way, and on and on and on. That gave me great bat control and great hand-eye coordination.

Pepper to me is like a slow game of batting practice. You don't hit it hard, you just use your bat control. It's good for your wrists. I played pepper with the batboys all the time. If you're in uniform and it's not time to take the field, why not play pepper?

Players today don't understand the value of pepper, if you do it right. You hit one to the guy on the right, then one to the guy on the left, then one to the guy in the middle. I think it's better than hitting off a tee, which is what the guys do today. I still can't figure out why they hit off a tee. What does that do for you? I don't remember a guy ever putting a ball on a tee for you in a game.

I was on track for the 1968 batting title as we moved into mid-June. I went 5 for 5 against the Atlanta Braves on June 18, raising my league-leading average to .363. I was scoring a lot of runs, and on my way to a league-high 210 hits that season. The bottom line is I was helping my team win. "I've got to agree with the general consensus around the league," said Braves manager Luman Harris. "Somehow, that Rose keeps figuring a way to beat you—with his bat, his speed, or his glove."

I loved playing in LA because Dodger Stadium was always packed, and as a player you wanted the electricity and excitement of playing in front of a big crowd, but there were issues with that ballpark. In those days, everyone was a victim of the lights at Dodger Stadium—third and first basemen were constantly losing hoppers to them. The stands of lights weren't located properly, so to fix the problem they took some of them down. After that you couldn't see well at home plate and there were shadows. That July I lost a ball in the lights at Dodger Stadium, and then busted my thumb diving to try to make a play.

I couldn't swing a bat with a broken thumb, so there was no way I could play, and they had to put me on the twenty-one-day disabled list. Three weeks out of the lineup, that was a nightmare for me, and the timing of the injury meant I'd miss the All-Star Game, even though I was the leading vote-getter in the National League.

By the All-Star break, Matty Alou of the Pittsburgh Pirates was leading the league in hitting at .331 and I was two points back at .329. Even with my busted thumb, I was still playing pepper in July. We were in Pittsburgh later that month and I was out in left field before the game, playing pepper with my thumb sticking out so it wouldn't get hurt any worse. Dave Bristol saw what I was doing.

"Can you hold the bat out there like you are playing pepper?" he asked me.

"Sure," I said.

"Let's put some kind of brace on your thumb, and you might be able to get in the lineup," he said.

So the first day I was eligible to come off the DL, we were in New York to play against the Mets at Shea Stadium and Dave put me back in the game—all because he'd seen me playing pepper. I had to wear a special brace, and my thumb was still busted and hurt like hell if it was cold, but I was back in the game.

A few days later, we swept a doubleheader over the Phillies, with George Culver tossing a no-hitter in the second game. Here's how the papers summed up my contribution: "Cincinnati scored three runs in each of the third and fourth innings. Pete Rose started both rallies with singles. The Reds took the opener when Rose tripled in the ninth and scored on Vada Pinson's sacrifice fly. Rose then saved the game by throwing out [Richie] Allen, who tried to score from second base on John Callison's two-out single." But even with two wins, we were in third place in the National League, fourteen games behind the Cardinals.

I was doing everything I could to help us win, and it bugged me that we were going to miss the playoffs again. I batted .471 for the month of August. I was determined to win that batting title, but Matty Alou wasn't making it easy on me. With two games left, we were at home against the Giants, facing Gaylord Perry. The Pirates, Matty's team, were in Chicago, facing Fergie Jenkins, who was trying to win his twentieth game of the season. Each of us had to deal with a great pitcher that day. Matty went 4 for 4 in the Pirates' loss that day, and Fergie was a twenty-game winner for the second straight season, a string he would run to an incredible six seasons in a row.

And what did I do against Gaylord, that crafty spitball artist? Through four at bats I was 4-for-4, just like Matty, even though Gaylord was throwing me nothing but spitballs. I remember hitting one ball and I swear to God, I watched the ball hit the bat and I could see the spit fly. But that didn't bother me. You expected that from Gaylord, and you respected him, because he was a hell of a competitor.

When I got my fourth hit, Gaylord glared at me.

"You got enough yet?" he yelled over to me.

"Not if I get another at bat," I told him honestly.

I came up again in the bottom of the ninth and made it 5 for 5, so Matty and I went a combined 9 for 9 that day with the batting title on the line. I was at .3354 going into the last game of the season and Matty was at .3339.

All I had to do on the last day of the season was do at least as well as Matty and I'd have my first batting title.

I doubled my first time up and then couldn't get a hit the rest of the day. But I was in luck: Matty went 0 for 4. I'd done it. I'd won my first batting title on the last day of the season. I was the first switch batter to win the National League hitting title since Pete Reiser of the Brooklyn Dodgers in 1941.

PETE ROSE GRABS NL BATTING TITLE was the headline in papers all across the country.

"I love the game," I told reporters afterward. "I love everything about it. Nothing in life is more fun. Baseball enables me to meet people. I enjoy that. I go to the ballpark every day, sign autographs, talk to reporters. I enjoy that."

As much as I hated going on the disabled list, I can say now that those three weeks gave me the second wind that I needed to have a closeout season. That's the truth of it, but at the time I never convinced myself of that, because the last thing I wanted to do was make a habit of taking three weeks off in the middle of every summer.

I figured that the batting title was going to come in handy in my next contract negotiations, when I pushed for the salary I was sure I deserved: $100,000. It might sound unbelievable to the contemporary fan, with multi-year contracts being so common now, but when I was a player we didn't have that. I had nothing but one-year contracts for my first sixteen seasons in the big leagues, all with the Reds. If you made the All-Star team or won a batting title, that helped your bargaining position to push for a raise.

"Imagine making a hundred grand for doing something you were happy to do for nothing when you were a kid," I told reporters. Not bad for a guy who started out as a skinny little kid no one thought had a future.

That year I came in second place in the voting for National League MVP, behind only Bob Gibson. You always hate to come in second in anything, but Bob Gibson had the kind of season you see once in a generation. He started 34 games and had 28 complete games. Imagine that in today's game. His ERA was 1.12, barely 1 run allowed per 9 innings, and he was 22–9 with a league-leading 13 shutouts and 268 strikeouts. He set a single-game strikeout record in the World Series with 17, but the Cardinals still lost to the Tigers in 7 games. Bob was the most competitive player I ever went against, and he was a master of intimidation. He never talked to you when he played against you. Nowadays when I see him he never stops talking! He's the nicest, friendliest guy you could ever want to meet.

The National League was loaded with top-notch starting pitchers in those days. You would fly out to LA and have to go against Koufax, Drysdale, and Sutton, three future Hall of Famers, and then you would go up north to San Francisco and you'd have Gaylord Perry and Juan Marichal waiting for you. Then you went to St. Louis and took your chances against Gibson and Steve Carlton, and in New York you were liable to face Seaver, Koosman, and Matlock.

Marichal had to have been the best pitcher I faced, even though I hit .340 off him. He was a real gamer and had five pitches he could throw for a strike at any given time. I think pitching at Candlestick Park helped him, too, with the wind blowing and the cold air and guys shivering and wishing they were somewhere else.

CHAPTER 17

Morganna

One time in the late 1960s my agent called me up and told me a man named Joe McCoy wanted me to come over to Pikeville, Kentucky, and make an appearance at a family banquet they were having, about four hours away from Cincinnati. Some of my family on my mother's side came from Kentucky, and I always felt like I had Kentucky in my blood. I said sure. I pulled up at the address they had given me and I couldn't believe how many Rolls Royces I saw out front and, once I went inside, how many Rolexes and diamonds I saw. This was a gathering of the famous McCoy family of Kentucky, and Joe McCoy and I hit it off right away.

The McCoys were just hardworking, down-to-earth folks—in other words, my kind of people. They made a lot of money, but they were good ol' boys. They were famous for their family history. A century earlier violence had broken out between the McCoys and another Appalachian family, the Hatfields, and one thing had led to another. Soon they had a full-blown feud on their hands. It went from generation to generation, getting passed down. To me that story was all about determination. Those families were stubborn and tough in the way that I was on a baseball field. I saw some of myself in them and I think they saw some of themselves in me. They used to talk about how the war between the Hatfields and McCoys went on forever.

When I first got to know Joe McCoy, the family was raking in a lot of money, mostly in the coal business. Joe had built a field house and sports complex in Phelps, Kentucky. Joe's son David was a basketball player, and he wanted him and the other kids in the area to have a good place to play games. They asked me to come down to be part of the first baseball game at the new complex and I was happy to make the drive over and throw out the first pitch.

Joe's brother Jim, a former Marine Corps sergeant, ran the mine, and one time they decided to take me down for a look-see. That was my first time in a coal mine and I had no idea what to expect. I'm riding on a track a quarter-mile deep into a tunnel, and it's as black as Hades down there. I could only see right in front of me with the little light shining from the top of my helmet. I'm not gonna lie, I was kind of scared. As I rolled along, every fifty feet or so there was a light, and then I went past that and it was all ink-black again. I was just trying to stay calm and not hyperventilate. You can't panic down there, because once you start in on panic, you might not stop.

Suddenly, there was a loud BOOM. The tunnel was shaking all around me, especially up above. Dust exploded at me from all directions at once and it was a gritty, gravelly kind of dust.

Oh my God, I was thinking to myself. *I'm going to be trapped under this fucking mountain.*

They were messing with me. They hadn't told me they were doing any mining that day, because they wanted to see how I'd react to a dynamite explosion. We got to the back of the mine and I watched them work, loading up the conveyor belt with lumps of coal, which scooted out of there to where they loaded it up on trucks and drove it away. Those were some hardworking people, really putting their backs into it.

I felt so comfortable over in that mine, it kind of reminded me of what made me tick as a ballplayer, which was being the hardest-working guy out there every inning of every game I played. It also reminded me of how lucky I was to being playing the game I loved for a living—instead of having to spend my work days hunched over in a hole in the ground hoping I didn't hear a big BOOM any second. I'd won my first batting title in 1968 and I came back the next season looking to make it two years in a row. We'd finished in fourth place two seasons in a row and we felt '69 was our year to win it all. I'd won the batting title by knowing who I was as a hitter. When you're a kid, there's nothing you want more than to impress everyone with a home run, but by the time I was in high school I knew the long ball was not my game, and I was totally focused on making myself the best contact hitter I could be. I had my share of extra-base hits and set my share of records, but my mission every time up at bat was to go with a pitch and take what was given to me.

It all started with being hungry up there. You went up to bat with an attitude that you were ready to feast on whatever pitching you'd be facing. Being a hungry hitter meant never being satisfied, and I tell kids that today. That's why I have the record today for two-hit games, I've got the record for three-hit games, I've got the record for four-hit games, and I've got the record for five-hit games. If I got two hits, I wanted three. If I had three, I wanted four. If I had four, I wanted five. I was always greedy. I always wanted more. I wish I could sit here and tell you that out of the sixteen thousand times I batted, I was able to bear down hard every time. No one could do that. But I guarantee I was able to bear down more than anyone else ever did.

I believed that if I could get on base, I'd be helping my team the best I could, since often I'd come around and score a run—and runs are the basic unit of baseball, the foundation of everything. I didn't need no fancy thinking to know that. I also believed in respect— respect for the game and respect for the opposing players. I might see you as my enemy, I might be ready to do everything I could to beat you, but I could still have respect. I wasn't one to toss down my helmet after I struck out. I'd just wait until my next turn at bat and take another crack. Whitey Ford and Mickey Mantle made fun of me as Charlie Hustle, but hustling all the time meant I was putting pressure on the infielders and outfielders, and sometimes if you put pressure on them you'd catch a break. My dad always said to give 110 percent, all the time, and I never forgot that.

But even when I hustled, no matter how hard I tried sometimes, the game was just going to play a lot harder for me—and that was how it was through the early parts of the '69 season. By the middle of May, we were struggling as a team, a game under .500, and I was batting .283, which just wasn't going to cut it. On May 14, I was getting off the team bus, walking into the ballpark before a game, and two boys came running after me, wanting me to sign autographs.

"Who said people don't like .280 hitters?" I joked to a couple of reporters.

That was my way of joking about myself. Everyone knew I was miserable, but by late June I'd got it into gear. We beat the Giants 9–1 at home to move to 37–31 on June 27, and I went 2 for 4 to lift my average to .317. On July 15 we dropped the opening game of a double-header to the Braves, and Dave Bristol was so upset, he had a closed-door meeting afterward. That was just Dave. He wore his emotions on his sleeve. If you made a mental mistake, you could be sure he'd be yelling at you about that. In the second game, I went 4 for 5 to push my average to .326 and we won the game. By August 1 we were ten games over .500 and not only was I still hitting, with the average at .329, but the rest of the team was hitting, too. We'd started referring to ourselves as the Big Red Machine, and the name found its way into a newspaper article on July 15, 1969, when Bob Hertzel wrote in the *Cincinnati Enquirer* that artificial turf "would be an aid to their already potent offense that Manager Dave Bristol and his players like to refer to as 'The Big Red Machine.'" The name, until then only mentioned briefly in one wire-service story, kind of stuck.

I can't get up in front of a group and say the Big Red Machine was the best team ever. I'd like to, but I can't. One thing I can say is that we had to be the most entertaining team ever. We had home-run champions, RBI champions, base-stealing champions, a flamboyant manager in Sparky Anderson, a Gold Glove catcher, and other Gold Glove fielders. We had black stars, we had Latino stars, we had white stars, all in the Hall of Fame. Think about that. The 1927 Yankees were a great team, but they didn't have Latinos and they didn't have black guys. The Big Red Machine had a white Hall of Famer (Johnny

Bench), an African American Hall of Famer (Joe Morgan), a Latino Hall of Famer (Tony Perez), and a manager in the Hall (Sparky).

REDS THINK HITTING was the headline on a wire-service story that went out at the start of that month. We were leading the league with a .285 average, leading the league in homers with more than 100, and instead of being the only .300 hitter on the team, I was one of six.

The writer, Lee Mueller, spent more time describing me on a baseball field than maybe anyone before or since.

"The legs of Pete Rose, wrapped tight in his gray Cincinnati Reds uniform, rock back and forth in the batting cage, his spikes pawing the earth, raking it, plowing it, cultivating it," Mueller wrote. "'Getitover!' he snaps, smashing one of batting practice pitcher Joe Nuxhall's wide throws into the gray dirt in front of him. He pounds home plate with his bat. Smash. 'Getitover!' Smash. 'Getitover!'

"Physically, Rose has been compared to several inanimate objects: Fireplugs, tree stumps and a stack of bowling balls with a crew cut. Nothing about Rose, however, is inorganic. At five foot ten, 190 pounds, he is all muscle, all motion, all desire. Waiting his turn in batting practice, he paces behind the cage, holding his bat, looking at it, gripping it, re-gripping it. The rage to hit that boils out of Pete Rose has become a flaming plague in Cincinnati, everybody has it."

The normal player didn't do the things that I did. But when they put the Big Red Machine together, and I was the oldest player, they all busted their asses, because it was contagious. Good, bad, or indifferent, it was contagious, and everyone busted their asses.

We had a very good August. We won 19 of 33 games to move to

72–58 and ended the month tied with the Giants for first place in the National League. A year earlier I'd hit .387 in August. This time, I batted .380. I only hoped I could avoid the September slump that struck me a year earlier.

Playing for my hometown team and starting September in first place—this was everything I'd dreamed about all through my childhood. We have always had great fans in Cincinnati, but that year as the team started to show signs of getting better, people were even more excited. They were into it.

We had a doubleheader at home against the Giants on September 8, and in the first game we took an early lead against Juan Marichal and hung on to win. I had two hits to push my average to .344. The second game ended up going into extra innings when the Giants scored three runs late to tie it up, and we finally won it in fifteen innings to pull off the sweep.

That was when I had first met Morganna, who had run out into the outfield at Crosley Field on a dare and created quite a commotion. She was the kind of woman who got attention wherever she went. Her measurements were 44½–27–32. As she later explained to a newspaper reporter, "All the players would look at me and whistle, all except Pete Rose, Reds' outfielder. He never noticed. One day a nice couple sitting behind me said, 'Why doesn't Pete notice you? Does he wear eye shadow or something?' So I leaped over the wall and ran on the field and kissed him. I think he liked it."

I was heading out to the outfield to take my position, and you know how you feel when somebody is behind you? It was like that, which made no sense at all. Who could be behind me in the outfield?

I turned around to take a look, and all I could see were these big tits flopping around as a woman ran after me. I kept running, to stay ahead of her, but then I ran out of outfield.

"Honey, you're going to get in a lot of trouble," I told her.

"I sure in hell hope so," she said.

Then she planted one on me. She gave me a big kiss in front of all the fans at the ballpark, and security came out and escorted her off the field. Morganna was from Kentucky and I was the first baseball player she went after and kissed on the field. After that it became a thing. She'd go on the field and kiss players and get attention in the media. She got so famous after that she was on with Johnny Carson.

But back then it was all new. The day of that doubleheader with the Giants, I drove across the river afterward to go see her at her strip club, called the Brass Ass. I arrived too late to catch her act onstage. I went backstage, and she was sitting back there in the dressing room signing pictures for guys in Vietnam. We talked a little, I gave her some roses, and we became friends after that.

I was driving home after visiting Morganna, and by then it was around midnight. I was coming up on a yellow light and was pretty sure I got through it before it turned red, but a police officer disagreed. He pulled me over. Well, the next thing I knew, I was down at the police station, it was all taking a lot of time, and I didn't get home to bed until probably 2:30 A.M.

The next day, my mom woke up and saw my picture on the cover of one of the local papers, and thought for sure I'd been killed. They made it out like I was in major trouble, having run a red light—which I really didn't—and coming in after curfew—which I really didn't, either. We were back at home the next day against the Giants, and this time we were facing Gaylord Perry, well known for throwing a spitball.

"Perry, of course, has been in the center of numerous spitball incidents," as one newspaper put it that year. "He's been searched, stopped, and criticized. Always fidgety on the mound, the lanky right-hander makes a ritual of going to his mouth, his neck, and his cap with his right hand."

There was a promotion that night for Knodel-Tygrett, a local company that made TVs, and the first twenty thousand fans who came in all got a little rubber ball. Now I had a lot of respect for Gaylord Perry. We knew what was coming—that was just how it was with Gaylord—but when he threw seventeen spitballs in the first inning, it was just too much for me. They were never going to stop Gaylord from throwing the spitball, but the umpires had to at least make a show of asking for a ball to inspect now and then. This umpire, a rook umpire, Andy Olsen, hadn't done that.

As I was walking back out to the outfield after I grounded out in the first, I walked right past Olsen and gave him an earful.

"Why don't you do your fucking job?" I asked the ump. "Why don't you check the ball once in a while? Any blind so-and-so can see a spitball."

Olsen just stared back at me. Then, as I was running out to my position, another ump on that crew decided to eject me. I couldn't believe it. For what? Olsen and I started jawing pretty good, and Dave Bristol ran out to help me yell back. Olsen was pissed.

"He started poking me in the chest and telling me that he'd do his job and that I should start doing mine," I explained to reporters at the time.

But remember, we had twenty thousand fans who'd all been given a little rubber ball for a promotion, and those rubber balls all came bouncing down on the field about then. The fans threw them in protest of me getting kicked out of the game.

The next day's *Cincinnati Enquirer* had the headline UMP FLUNKS SALIVA TEST. I couldn't have put it better myself!

That was a rare hitless night for me. I was getting my knocks, and on September 23 I went 3 for 5 in each game of a doubleheader with the Dodgers, putting me at .344. All year long, I'd been back and forth with Roberto Clemente of the Pirates, a great hitter, and our competition was the talk of baseball. I went 0-for-3 against the Astros on September 28 and dropped my average to .347, just ahead of Clemente (.341) and the Mets' Cleon Jones (.340). Even *The New York Times* took note, with the headline ROSE KEEPS BATTING LEAD.

Our last game of the season was in Atlanta on October 2. I went into that game with a .348 average, just ahead of Clemente (.342). I figured I needed one hit to make sure I won the title, and that one hit just wouldn't come. I was 0 for 1, then 0 for 2, and finally 0 for 3. It was killing me. Finally, in the eighth inning, I was going to get one more shot at it.

As I was reaching into the dugout for my bat, a fan in the front row at Atlanta Stadium told me that Clemente was 3 for 3 that day. He and I were basically tied for the lead. I was as nervous as I've ever been on a baseball field. Tony Perez had put us ahead with a three-run homer in the seventh, so I didn't have to worry about winning the game, just getting on base. There were two outs and runners at second and third, a situation where I'd never in my life bunted. No one would be expecting a bunt and I was ahead in the count, 1–0. So I dropped one down the line, it rolled about forty feet, and I ran like hell. And I beat the throw.

"That was the biggest hit I ever got," I told Dave Bristol afterward. "Not the longest, the biggest."

He and I laughed later at the idea that I would possibly have taken myself out of the lineup that day to protect my lead and claim the hitting title. "Someone suggested that Pete sit out the game," Bristol said at the time. "Pete said nothing doing. I would have pushed him up myself but he's not that kind of guy. You don't have to push him."

We'd missed out on first place again. The Braves and Mets were headed for the playoffs and we were headed home. For me it had been a strong season. I won the batting title on the last day of the season for the second year in a row, and I'd edged out the great Roberto Clemente. As I said at the time, "It's an honor to beat out Clemente. He's the best hitter in baseball."

My goal was always to have 200 hits and score 100 runs, and I'd finished with 218 hits and a league-leading 120 runs. I'd also hit for some power, finishing with 11 triples, 16 homers, and 82 RBIs, all career highs for me.

That was also the first year that I won a Gold Glove Award. Not too many second basemen turned third basemen turned left fielder turned right fielder won the Gold Glove, and consider this: the previous six seasons, the National League had the same three Gold Glove winners in the outfield, and what a trio it was—Roberto Clemente, Curt Flood, and Willie Mays. In 1969 it was Clemente, Flood, and Pete Rose. I won the Gold Glove by displacing Willie Mays, who might be the greatest all-around outfielder who ever lived. Living up to the advice from scout Slugger Blomski, in 1969 I'd played 101 games in right field, fifty-six in center field, and two at second base. How did I win the Gold Glove that year? I didn't have anything like the arm of a Roberto Clemente. So what did I do? I charged the ball hard, running as fast as I could, and then I hit the cutoff man. It's amazing how often good things happen in the game of baseball when you charge the ball and hit the cutoff man.

CHAPTER 18

Collision

Crosley Field was the home of baseball for me, my idea of the pinnacle. The place had its quirks, but it was less than seven miles from where I grew up, and I loved playing there. For my buddies and me, for my dad and my brother, Crosley Field felt like it belonged to us. So I had some mixed emotions about playing my last game there in June 1970. Starting June 30, we'd be playing our games at a new stadium, built of concrete, called Riverfront Stadium.

I remember my new manager, Sparky Anderson, actually gave me the lineup card for the last game we played at Crosley Field that June, which was a great honor. We were winning and we were playing exciting baseball with a team full of young up-and-comers. The fans loved it.

For the 4,543rd and final National League game to be played at Crosley Field, we came from behind to beat Juan Marichal and the Giants, thanks mostly to home runs by Johnny Bench and Lee May. I chipped in myself. Here was how *Dayton Daily News* sports editor Si Burick described it: "Rose came up in the fifth with the team behind, 4–2, and bounced a double off Marichal's shin. But this was no ordinary double. It was a carom shot past the second baseman and into short right field. To beat the throw to second Pete took a belly whopper slide that must have started twenty feet from the bag. The only other man in the park, indeed the only other in baseball who could have done the same, was Willie Mays of the losers."

My dad had told me as a kid to play like Pepper Martin, known for his headfirst slides, and I made that my trademark. Sliding headfirst, you could keep your eyes on the ball and use your hands to avoid the tag. I never did figure out why they called it a belly whopper. I used to get strawberries on my elbows and my knees. Some parks were worse than others. It was tough in Pittsburgh and Atlanta because those were such hard fields. Sliding headfirst at Candlestick Park had its own issues. Because of the wind, they used to water the field every three innings. Sliding headfirst at Candlestick one night, I got stuck in the mud and came up three feet short. One time at the Astrodome I was wearing a vest and slid headfirst so hard that the whole vest tore off at the top and went down like I was wearing a diaper.

Sparky had a great sense of humor. Everyone was sharing their memories of Crosley Field and this was what he told reporters at the time: "When I played here for the Phils in '59, this was the only park where they put the batting averages up. Mine was always like .146. It was very embarrassing."

I wasn't happy in October 1969 when the Reds fired manager Dave Bristol. I loved playing for Dave, and called him as soon as I heard the news to tell him how much I'd miss going to battle with him. Sparky was named as his successor in December, and I felt it was a good choice. I'd keep an open mind and get to know my new skipper. The day he took over as manager, I walked up to him and shook his hand.

"I know I'm the highest-paid player on this team," I told him, "but I'll do anything I can for the Cincinnati Reds. You can count on me."

I played for a lot of good managers, but Sparky was the best. He was the most street-smart guy I've ever been around, and he understood players. He understood what made them tick. Sparky was calm, cool, and collected. He wasn't a red-ass manager the way Dave was. If you made a mistake, Sparky would kind of just let it roll. But if you made the same mistake again, he'd call you into his office for a low-key private talk.

I was a terrible spectator during a baseball game. When Sparky didn't play me, I'd drive him nuts! I'd stand right next to him the whole time. He'd trip over me every time he tried to move. I'd say, "Sparky, what are you going to do here? Who are you going to put in there?" It drove him crazy. Finally he'd say, "Get the heck out there!" I wasn't down at the end loading up on bubble gum. I was sitting right there watching him give signs to the first-base coach or the third-base coach. That's how I learned to manage, watching Sparky all those years.

It took Sparky time to figure out what made us tick. When you're a baseball manager, this is crucial, since you're asking players to go to war with you day in and day out. You need to know who you can count on and how they'll react. Who wants to bat with a man on third and two outs? Who wants to be brought into the game with bases loaded and one out and you need a strikeout? Some guys don't want that situation. Others are hungry for it.

By the All-Star break, we were the hottest team in baseball. No other team had more than 55 wins going into the break, but our record was 62–26, a winning percentage of .705. The first game at Riverfront Stadium sold out beforehand, and there was a lot of excitement in town.

"The people of this city are never going to be described as blasé," wrote the *Dayton Daily News*. "Other cities in the country have an All-Star Game and you hardly know it. Here you know."

There was also a certain amount of chaos on that first game day. The new stadium wasn't quite ready, but we didn't let that slow us down. It was definitely an adjustment. Game time was about 8 P.M., and I arrived in front of Riverfront at quarter to four and was looking for a way in—it was all new to me!—when I saw Bowie Kuhn, the commissioner of baseball, also looking lost.

"How do you get in, Pete?" the commissioner asked me.

"I'm about to find out myself," I said.

We kept walking until we found an opening and ended up in the upper level of the stands. Some guy on a motor scooter came over to us and tried to throw us out.

"You'll have to get out of here until the gates open," he told us.

"Wait a minute," I told him. "This is the commissioner of baseball."

The commissioner laughed it off later. "I didn't expect him to recognize me, but when he didn't recognize Pete Rose, I knew we were in trouble," he said.

The place looked beautiful. I wasn't thrilled to be playing on AstroTurf, but they spent $50 million on the new stadium and everyone was excited. Before the game, the sellout crowd gave huge ovations, especially for Tony Perez, Johnny Bench, and me, and also for Henry Aaron of the Braves. However, not everything went smoothly, especially not the result: Aaron hit the first home run at Riverfront and the Braves won easily. I went 3 for 4 and Sparky got kicked out of the game for arguing with an umpire, his first ejection since taking over as Reds manager.

STADIUM DEBUT A LARGE FLOPEROO was the headline in the next day's *Dayton Journal Herald.* "There were the usual problems that go with opening a new park," Bucky Albers wrote. "The dirt on the pitching mound and batter's box was too soft. Atlanta starter Pat Jarvis fell down several times after delivering his pitches. . . . The new electric scoreboard had its problems, too. Its figures were erased completely a couple of times, and maybe it was just as well. The Reds were getting tired of looking at the sad news it carried."

There was a lot of work to do, since that year's All-Star Game was scheduled for Riverfront Stadium just two weeks later. Around then I talked to my friend "Sudden" Sam McDowell on the phone. Sam was a big kid from Pittsburgh, a pitcher for the Indians, and he'd be in town for the All-Star Game, playing for the American League. We made a plan to go out to dinner the night before the game with our wives.

About a week before the All-Star Game Sam called me again. "Ray Fosse was added to the roster, and he catches for me," he said. "Can he go to dinner with us?"

"Sure, why not?" I said.

The more the merrier, right? Ray had just been married that April and would bring along his wife, too. I took everyone out to dinner at a great place down on the river, near where I'd grown up, called the Sycamore Shores and Boat Club—famous for its Friday Seafood Smorgasbord.

Now, I liked this kid Ray Fosse just fine. He was twenty-three at the time, a first-round pick out of Marion, Illinois, who in his first full season in the big leagues was hitting .312, the best on the Indians, and doing such a good job behind the plate, he'd be the Gold Glove catcher for the American League that year. I liked Ray just fine, but I liked my buddy Sam McDowell more. I'd have been happy if it was just Sam and me and our wives. Instead, it was the six of us, and Ray had a lot of questions for me, mostly about our young catcher, Johnny Bench.

I knew all about Johnny, who I'd taken under my wing when he joined the Reds. Ray asked every question in the world about Johnny Bench, and I did my best to give him good answers. I've always tried to help out young players, like I helped Ralph Garr and Dusty Baker when I gave them my leisure suits. I was just trying to help out a young kid. We had a great dinner and then went back to my place and had another drink or two. By then we were all friends, and when Sam started playing the guitar, I even sang along. We had ourselves a good time, but we wrapped up by 1 A.M. and I drove them back to the team hotel.

The next day was the All-Star Game and it was a great moment in my life because my dad was able to attend the game. He'd seen me win Rookie of the Year, he'd seen me win back-to-back batting titles, and now he was going to watch in person as I played an All-Star Game in front of a crowd of 51,838 fans in Cincinnati.

Another thing I remember about the game was that my old friend Morganna, the stripper, did her best to get down on the field to come give me a kiss. She knew what she was doing at Crosley Field, but it was hard to get down on the field at Riverfront, which had just opened, and she got kind of caught up going over the rail. They grabbed her, and pictures were taken of this one cop grabbing hold of one of her tits. They made a big deal out of that, because the picture was in the paper, but she was harmless. She owned a minor league baseball team later in life! Ain't that America?

A lot of guys look at the All-Star Game as some kind of party or charade. That kind of attitude pissed me off. I played as hard as I could every time I was on a baseball field, from Knothole League baseball as a kid to the minor leagues to the big leagues to the All-Star Game. The way I saw it was: there's no difference between an All-Star Game and a spring training game and a World Series game. The reason for that is simple. Let me spell it out: F-A-N-S. The fans pay good money to come see you play and have every right to expect you'll bust your ass, no matter what kind of game it is. That was the way I always thought of it and what I always told anyone who asked.

When you play in an All-Star Game, you feel like you are at the center of the universe. Before the game started, who did they bring out to throw out the first pitch but the president of the United States, Richard M. Nixon! The president put on a glove—he loved sports—and made a looping little throw to Johnny Bench, and then made another to the American League catcher, Bill Freehan of the Tigers, and then he just kept throwing—tossing balls to three fans at various points in the crowd at Riverfront.

It turned out to be a hell of a good game. Tom Seaver and Jim Palmer both pitched three innings of shutout ball to open the game, and it was scoreless until the sixth when Ray Fosse, my companion at dinner the night before, hit a line-drive single to right field off Gaylord Perry, moved to second on a sacrifice bunt by my other dinner companion, Sam McDowell, and then scored on Carl Yastrzemski's single. Frank Robinson, then with the Orioles, grounded out to end the inning and keep it 1–0 American League.

Then in the seventh, Ray came up again with the bases loaded, again facing Gaylord Perry, who couldn't really throw his spitball in the All-Star Game as often as he did at other times. Brooks Robinson was on third, Tony Oliva on second, and Davey Johnson on first. Ray hit the ball to deep center field and missed the home run, but did score Brooks Robinson with a sacrifice fly to make it 2–0.

I'd walked in the sixth inning and by the time I led off the eighth inning for us, we were behind 4–1. I was a guy who hated to strike out. I'd struck out only sixty-five times all season long in more than seven hundred plate appearances, but at the 1970 All-Star Game, Jim Perry struck me out.

We came up in the bottom of the ninth, still down 4–1, and rallied to tie it. Dick Dietz homered, and then Bud Harrelson and Joe Morgan added singles, all off Catfish Hunter. Then Willie McCovey singled off Fritz Peterson to make it 4–3, and Roberto Clemente hit a sacrifice fly off Mel Stottlemyre to knot it up at 4–4. I was up next and, would you believe it, with the game on the line, the chance to win the game right there—two outs, bottom of the ninth—I struck out again and we went on to extra innings.

The crowd was kind of quiet by the time I came up again with two outs in the bottom of the twelfth. Clyde Wright had taken care of both Joe Torre and Roberto Clemente on groundouts. No way I was striking out three times.

"For Chrissake, Ray, give me something I can foul tip," I said to Fosse behind the plate. "I haven't hit the ball yet."

He just laughed. Clyde Wright missed, and missed again, for a 2–0 count. I was sure he would come in with a fastball, and when he did, I lined it to center for a single, then took second on Billy Grabarkewitz's single to left. Jim Hickman was up next, and with two outs, I'd be running on anything—as fast as I could.

Hickman singled to center and I hauled ass. Amos Otis was out in center, charging the ball to make a throw, and our third-base coach, Leo Durocher, was waving me on. I never hesitated. I knew it was going to be close and I could win the game for us right there and make a lot of Cincinnati fans happy.

Otis made a decent throw, but it was up the line toward third. Fosse had to come out from behind home plate to make a play on it. So for Fosse, the ball and the base runner—me—were arriving at the same time, and the ball was sinking before it got to Ray. He was going to have to short-hop the ball, which is a tough play. If Otis had got enough on the throw for it to travel another foot or two, then Ray would have caught the ball cleanly and I'd have been out.

I started to go into my headfirst slide, but Ray had the plate blocked, with his feet spread, so I couldn't slide headfirst and be safe. I'd break both my collarbones. Instead I went over him and tagged the plate with the palm of my outstretched right hand. I actually had the advantage in that situation, and I knew it. Ray couldn't give his total concentration to two things at once. He had to focus on the ball to try to catch it cleanly, and that meant he couldn't keep track of me. So I had the element of surprise. As it happened, I hit him just before the ball got there. I did what I always did and what I'd do again today if I had the same situation: I ran right over him just like anyone would expect the son of a sandlot football legend to do. That's always been the way I play the game. The ball hit off Ray, but barreling down from third the way I was, the game on the line, I couldn't see that. My knee hit his shin guard.

"You OK, Ray?" I said once the play was over, bending over to talk to him.

"Yeah," he said.

Leo Durocher was out there by then. Then Dick Dietz, who had been on deck, was out there. All the players were coming out because it was the end of the game. I never wanted to hurt anyone and I had nothing at all against Ray. He had to go in for X-rays on his left shoulder after the game, and no question he was in pain, but two days later he was back in the lineup, catching for the Indians. So I felt better about him. As for me, I was too banged up after that collision to play our next game, or our next game after that, or the next one, either. I missed three games. But Fosse didn't miss a game.

Later people tried to say that I was playing dirty, or that I wanted to hurt Ray. I was playing straightforward, hard-nosed baseball, and Ray and everyone else knew it. This was the analysis in the next day's *New York Times*, as good a source as any, I reckon: "On Hickman's hit, a liner to center, Rose came racing around from second and crashed into Ray Fosse, the American League catcher, just as a surprising throw from Amos Otis was arriving. Fosse suffered a badly bruised left shoulder, Rose a badly bruised left thigh, but both reported today that their injuries were not that serious."

The article continued: "Some American Leaguers questioned the 'necessity' of Rose's body block, but their manager, Earl Weaver of

Baltimore, promptly characterized it as a proper hard play. 'I thought Rose got there a little ahead of the ball,' he said, 'and Fosse was trying to block the plate. They both did what they had to do.'"

"I don't know," Fosse said that night. "Some guys on the bench thought he could have gone around me. I don't know. It's the way he runs. He's got to score it any way he can, I guess."

Ray had that right. It was just unfortunate, because I got to him before the ball did. He made a hell of a play to even do what he did. I give him credit for that. He did his job and I did mine. Neither of us did anything wrong.

Dick Young, the highly opinionated *New York Daily News* columnist, offered this take: "They argued it in the clubhouses and later in press headquarters. They are arguing it now, in offices, in clubs, in bars. Was it a dirty play, or was it just good, hard baseball? . . . Pete Rose was a nice guy. Now he is in the center of a controversy. Now there is a little dirt on him."

I was in the trainer's room after the game with an ice pack on my knee, and Rusty Staub stopped in to see how I was feeling.

"Hot damn, if it ain't Sarah Bernhardt!" he said.

That's how ballplayers are, always giving each other a hard time, but I wasn't acting then, and I wasn't acting the next three games when I couldn't play. I hated to miss even one game. Who knew how many hits you might have had that day, hits you could never get back if you were out of the lineup?

That was a great baseball game and it was a great finish. I loved winning the game. To me baseball was always a battle, and sometimes you had to battle to win in ways that looked rough. I think after that my image was even more that of a winner—a little bit of a roughneck, maybe, in a baseball sense, but a guy completely committed to finding a way to beat you, and that's who I was all right. The rules were on my side. It was a damn shame that Ray's shoulder was banged up on the play, and bothered him for years after that, but I always believed that in my shoes, Ray would have done just what I did.

How you saw that play had a lot to do with who you were rooting for in the game, if you were rooting at all. By the end of the month, I'd received so many letters about that collision with Ray, I had a pile half as tall as my locker. I opened each and every one. As I told a reporter at the time, "National League fans think I did what I had to do, while American League fans think I committed a terrible sin."

I had never played in a playoff or World Series game, so for a lot of baseball fans around the country, the annual All-Star Game was about the only chance they had to see me play. That play with Fosse made a lasting impression and defined me in their eyes for years to come. It made me Pete Rose. Back then you didn't have sports cable shows that gave highlights from around the league every night. People focused more on their own teams in their own markets.

Then all of a sudden, I was the hometown kid in Cincinnati, playing in prime time for a national audience watching live on TV, and the way it ended, with me bowling over the catcher, because that was my style of play, that kind of opened up the gates for me. The fans in Cincinnati knew my style already, but the national audience wasn't aware of it up until that game.

Everything is timing in sports. You know how many times in my career I ran into a catcher at home plate? Umpteen times. But because it happened in an All-Star Game and everybody was watching, to this day, almost fifty years later, they show that play every year. That sequence became so famous, such a talked-about part of baseball lore, I've probably been asked about it hundreds or even thousands of times. Same goes for Ray, I'm sure. Some of those times I got a little impatient and answered in ways I shouldn't have.

No way was I trying to hurt Ray on that play. I'd had a great time the night before, talking with Ray and his wife—still married today, fifty years later—along with Sam and his wife. I was trying to win a baseball game, the way I did every time I stepped on the field. So was Ray Fosse, who was a hell of a player. No one ever told me you're not supposed to play like that in an All-Star Game. Ray and I will always be linked in baseball history, and I believe we can both take some pride in having battled that day in Cincinnati, having given our all. Ray was a star of the game, and in the end I was, too. Would I do the same thing again today in the same situation? Damn right I would. But would I rather it had all gone down without Ray having suffered an injury that would dog his career? You bet.

CHAPTER 19

"He Never Walks When He Can Run"

Once the 1970 All-Star break was behind us and we could focus on the rest of the season, it was clear where we were headed: to a World Series matchup with the Baltimore Orioles, who had lost to the New York Mets the previous October. Baltimore had a load of talent and a big lead in the American League, and we had a load of talent and a big lead in the National League. At the start of August, we had a twelve-game lead over the Dodgers in the National League West, playing .692 ball (72–32). The Orioles' cushion in the AL East was only six-and-a-half games, and the Minnesota Twins over in the AL West had a similar record at that point, but the Orioles had so much talent—ace Jim Palmer, Brooks "The Human Vacuum Cleaner" Robinson at third, and my old friend, future Hall of Famer Frank Robinson—plus a shrewd manager in Earl Weaver, and they were hungry after falling to the Mets in the '69 World Series.

We had a strong core of young players. At twenty-nine, I was like a big brother to some of these young kids coming up. Tony Perez was twenty-eight, Lee May twenty-seven, Bobby Tolan twenty-four,

and Johnny Bench just twenty-two. One of our pitchers, Don Gullett, was only nineteen years old. The Reds had taken him in the first
round of the 1969 draft out of McKell High in South Shore, Kentucky, a couple hours east of Cincinnati, and he was already getting
a shot in the big leagues. The kid impressed me by knowing when to
keep quiet.

"The fact is Don has little to say," noted the *Dayton Journal Herald*
in May 1970, "but it isn't from a lack of ability to communicate or,
more important, any shortage of intelligence. It's merely that he keeps
his eyes open and his mouth shut, a habit which many people today
lament as a rapidly disappearing trait among American youth."

Sparky, as ever, had a good read on the youngster. "Don is a lis-
tener, but underneath he's a real sharp kid," he said that month. "I
know he's a little awed at being around people like Pete Rose and
Tony Perez, but he's forming a lot of opinions about what he sees and
hears. I'll bet he'll always be the kind of fellow who makes up his
own mind about things."

We were so far ahead, it took people a while to notice we'd
slacked off a little. We played .500 ball (24–24) after the All-Star
break, going into September. By the middle of the month, we'd lost
three in a row, and Sparky—who always said he didn't believe in team
meetings—called us all in to fire up the team. I never needed firing
up, but I thought his timing was good.

"We've got to start proving again we can win," Sparky told us.
"I want you to go out and play these last thirteen games as though
we're just starting the season."

We all agreed it was a good speech, but we went out afterward and lost to the Houston Astros, 9–2. The game did have some value, though. I'd had my eye on an up-and-coming second baseman for Houston named Joe Morgan. He was yet another big leaguer from Oakland, California, like Frank Robinson and Vada Pinson and so many others I respected. Joe was only a couple years younger than me, but he'd been hurt and missed most of '68, and in '69 he batted just .236 after hitting .270 his first three full seasons in the bigs. Joe was an All-Star in '66 and again in '70.

Joe was my kind of ballplayer. He was smart, he played hard, and he was always one step ahead. In Houston that day after Sparky gave us the pep talk, I went out and played my ass off. Twice I smoked the ball up the middle and damned if Joe Morgan didn't find a way to range up the middle and rob me of a hit. Twice! Cesar Cedeno made a great catch in center, twisting up against the wall, to cost me a triple. Joe Morgan hit a ball down the right-field line in the third inning, just foul, and even though it was the Astrodome, I hauled ass after the ball and took a diving leap to try to catch it. I couldn't quite get it, and banged up my elbow slamming into a concrete wall. That was just how it was playing there, you couldn't let it slow you down. After the game one of my teammates asked me why I risked injury with a play like that and I said: "What do you think that meeting tonight was all about?"

I was always pushing the other guys to play a little harder, whether I said it that way or not, and usually I helped get them going. That day in Houston I reminded some of my teammates of how we had to play to be champions. It was all about doing the little things and the big things, about taking what you're given, about being a team player, and about always wanting to win at least a little more than the other team. I was still writing my regular column for the newspapers, and that summer I tried to set down my philosophy on hitting.

"If you try to hit the ball to three different fields, you have a better chance," I wrote, encouraging young kids learning the game to try to learn hitting from both sides of the plate. "When you make contact there are a lot of open holes in the infield and outfield."

I also emphasized the importance of being alert. "You must watch the pitched ball from the time it leaves the pitcher's hand," I wrote. "He's only sixty feet, six inches away from you and you don't have much time to make up your mind. I try to swing only at strikes and I pay strict attention to the pitcher when I'm in the on-deck circle. I try to pick up his pitching pattern to see if he throws two curves in a row or two fastballs in a row and how he mixes up his pitches. I try to watch what's going on out on the field. Your eyes can do a lot for you in baseball. I look for a fastball every pitch. I never look for a curve ball. Being ready for the fastball enables me to have time to adjust for the curve ball."

Home-run hitters are guess hitters. I never was. Guess hitters get hit a lot, because if you're guessing a slider low and away and the guy throws you a fastball up and in, you just got hit in the ribs. I was always studying the pitchers. That's why I had success against guys I saw a lot and often struggled facing guys I'd never seen. I didn't write down in a book what anybody threw. I wrote it down in my head. If I was going against Bob Gibson, I knew he was a fastball–slider pitcher and he went in and out, but I'm still not going to guess. You couldn't hit his fastball if you were guessing slider. If you're going to guess, I would recommend you guess fastball. As a switch batter, I was a good curveball hitter. Curveballs didn't fool me. Sliders were always coming in on me.

I had another chance to make my dad proud of me that September. We had a ceremony back at Boldface Park in Cincinnati, where I played all those games as a boy, right next to my grandma's house. They decided to rename it Pete Rose Field. There was a ceremony with me and Bill DeWitt, the Reds' owner, honoring us both for what we'd done to support Knothole Baseball, and I felt like my grandmother was looking out the window and keeping an eye on us the whole time.

We didn't finish the regular season strong. The Orioles finished the season with eleven straight wins, then swept the Twins in the playoffs to run their winning streak to fourteen games in a row. We were just 32–30 over our last sixty-two games, and the day before we opened our playoff series against the Pittsburgh Pirates at home, some wise-ass reporter was actually walking around the locker room asking players if they thought we were going to choke. Choke? Us?

The umpires were picketing outside Three Rivers Stadium during the first game of that series, and only 31,530 fans showed up. We didn't show up either—not for a while, anyway. Through nine innings we hadn't been able to score a single run off Dock Ellis. The good news was, Pittsburgh hadn't been able to touch Gary Nolan either. In the top of the tenth, Sparky decided to send up a pinch hitter for Nolan, and chose a thirty-one-year-old journeyman, Tyrone Cline, who we picked up at the trading deadline. Cline then ripped a double to right-center on a 1–2 slider, and did his best Pete Rose imitation, digging for three all the way, even with Roberto Clemente out in right field hurrying after the ball. Clemente might just have had the best throwing arm of anyone ever to play right, and he made a strong throw, but the ball and Cline arrived at the same time and Cline got in just under the tag. After that it was back to the top of the order, meaning me, and the Pirates had to bring in their infield and hope for a ground ball hit right at someone, so they'd have a play at the plate to avoid giving up the go-ahead run.

For me, batting with no outs, a runner at third, the infield drawn in, and the game on the line was like sitting down for a big, juicy steak. My mouth was almost watering, I was so hungry for it. I singled to right to bring in the run, then tagged up and moved to second on a Tony Perez deep fly, and came around to score on Lee May's double into the corner. We won it 3–0, then won an easy Game 2, and came home to make it three straight, giving the papers some extra days to trump up the coming World Series between the Orioles and Reds.

We all expected Frank Robinson, who had been such a great player for the Reds when I was coming up, to have a big series for Baltimore. He was thirty-five by then, the only player ever to be an MVP in both leagues, a twelve-time All-Star, and always a force. He played down the angle of wanting to beat up on his old team to show how wrong they were to trade him, a trade I'd been blunt about saying was a terrible move.

"I have a world of memories about Cincinnati and most of them are good," Frank told reporters at Riverfront Stadium. "But this place isn't Cincinnati to me. It would be a lot different if we were playing in Crosley Field or the man [Bill DeWitt] was still with the team or I had more friends left with the Reds."

Frank and I were always good friends, and they asked him if he'd be socializing with me during the series.

"No, I'd be afraid to go out to his house," Frank told them. "He had Ray Fosse out there the night before the All-Star Game and then tried to kill him." Old friends can kid each other like that.

One thing about the 1970 World Series: All the games were played in the afternoon. That was the last time that was true of a World Series, the last time kids who couldn't stay up late could still watch the whole game. So for Game 1 at Riverfront Stadium, the crowd was already nearing full strength by noon, an hour before game time. By the time the Jackson Five came out to sing the National Anthem, with the Lemon-Monroe High School Band in the outfield playing the music, the electricity in the new concrete ballpark was intense. Standing there looking out at that big American flag billowing in center field, I was proud to be a Red, proud to be a ballplayer, and proud to be giving my dad the thrill of his life, watching his son play in the World Series for the hometown Cincinnati fans. Little Michael Jackson, who was all of twelve years old, sounded good busting out "And the rockets' red glare / the bombs bursting in air."

The game opened with the Orioles going down in order against our starter, Gary Nolan, and then I led off the bottom of the inning by grounding out to shortstop. I was kicking myself back in the dugout, because Bobby Tolan tagged the Baltimore starter, young Jim Palmer, right after me with a double to right center; Tony Perez just missed a home run to right, which moved Tolan over to third; and then Johnny Bench singled to left to give us a 1–0 lead. Lee May then singled to left as well. The inning ended with Bernie Carbo lining out to third. The way the guys were hitting the ball, if I could have got on base to start it off, that would have been a big inning. Lee May made it 3–0 with a two-run homer in the bottom of the third. The Orioles came back on home runs by Boog Powell and Elrod Hendricks to tie it up, and then in the sixth inning came a screwy play. Bernie Carbo walked, and moved up to third on a Tommy Helms single, then looked ready to score when pinch hitter Ty Cline tapped one in front of the plate. Somehow the home plate umpire Ken Burkhart got in Ty's way and they had a collision, and then Burkhart, lying flat on the ground, called Ty out. As I said later, "The umpire was out—that's for sure."

If not for the collision, Ty would have been safe, but it was still frustrating, since it looked like the catcher tagged him with his glove and had the ball in his throwing hand. Burkhart made the only call he could, so the game was still tied. Brooks Robinson's solo shot an inning later put the Orioles up, and that was the final score. Again in Game 2 we jumped out early to a 3–0 lead and added to it, but Baltimore exploded for a five-run fifth and held on to win 6–5. We'd lost both games at home to start the series. No team in the sixty-seven-year history of the World Series had come back to win after losing the first two games.

I joked before the game, after watching Oriole third baseman Brooks Robinson, an absolute magician with the glove, that he could play third with pliers. Sure enough, Brooks's glove work made a huge difference in Game 3. I was 0 for 6 after two games and told the reporters I was going to have a stroke if I didn't get a hit. I led off Game 3 with a single to center, and Bobby Tolan moved me over with a bunt single. Tony Perez hit a hard chopper to the left side of the infield that had hit written all over it, but Brooks leaped and snagged the ball, stepped on third to force me, then threw to first for a double play. All day long Brooks Robinson was making amazing plays and when he came up in the sixth, the crowd at Memorial Stadium gave him a standing ovation. We lost 9–3.

"I told some of the writers after Tuesday's game that if I had known Brooks Robinson wanted a car that badly, Johnny Bench and I would have given him one," I wrote in the newspaper that week. "Every year the Lord picks out a guy who's the best player in the World Series and this year it looks like it's going to be him. . . . You saw again Tuesday how this is a game of inches. That first inning, if Tony Perez's ball is a hit rather than a double play, we might break the game open right there."

I was so worried we were going to get swept. That would have been murder on my father. That was all I kept thinking about, how hard it would be on my dad. The night before Game 4, I was sitting in the coffee shop of the Downtown Holiday Inn and started talking about him.

"You know who this is really hurting?" I asked Bob Hertzel, a reporter for the *Cincinnati Enquirer*. "It's hurting my dad worse than anyone, really. We can't lose four in a row for his sake. He takes it harder than anyone, and I can't stand to see him have it so tough. We've just got to win one, so he can show up at work. If we lose four in a row, they'll work him over so bad at work that he won't be able to sleep for a month."

We did finally win a game, taking Game 4 6–5, and Lee May and I both homered in that one, but other than avoiding a sweep, the game only bought us one more day. If we could have won the third game in Baltimore and sent the series back home to Cincinnati, we'd have all been confident about winning two straight to pull off one of the greatest comeback wins in sports. It wasn't to be. I doubled in the first inning of Game 5 and came around to score on a Johnny Bench single, part of a three-run rally for us that inning, but that was our scoring for the day and Baltimore hammered us 9–3 to win the World Series.

I hated losing that series. We were the better team. The morning after it was over, I picked up the *Dayton Journal Herald* and they had a picture of me on second, after my first-inning double, glaring at the world. The caption read "If only looks could kill here."

Below was the headline ROSE STILL BELIEVES REDS ARE THE BEST. (And I did, and I do.) Then again, another headline on that page read COOPERSTOWN WANTS BROOKS' MAGIC GLOVE. Two evenly matched teams had gone head to head and they'd gotten the momentum and beat us. That was all there was to it.

"Twice we had them 3–0 and another time 4–0 and they came back and beat us," I wrote in my column that week. "I don't think that's murdering us. I'm not going to blow up their pitching staff because they didn't impress me that much. In our league, we're used to smokers. They're all breaking-ball pitchers, and I don't mind breaking-ball pitchers. I'd rather hit against them than a Gibson, Marichal, or Singer. I still say ours is a better league."

I also vowed that we'd be back. "None of us think this is going to be our last World Series," I wrote.

In the *New York Daily News* that week, under the headline REDS EYE RETURN GO IN '71, Phil Pepe predicted in his first paragraph, "The Reds can come back next year. The Reds will come back next year."

That was the widespread feeling, but I'd been raised to fight for everything I got and to assume nothing. You never know when you're going to get back to the big one. Some guys get a taste early and never get back to the World Series their whole careers. We had a great young team; the Orioles made the most of the moment and we didn't.

Following the 1970 season, I went in to talk to Bob Howsam, the Reds' general manager, about a raise. Those one-year contract negotiations were never easy. It takes a lot to negotiate sixteen different contracts.

"You dropped thirty-two points in your batting average," he said. "And you didn't even lead the team in hitting."

"Who cares?" I said. "We won the pennant. We went to the World Series."

It was going to be a long wait for spring training and another season. I'd keep busy, the way I always did, and tour with my basketball team, wearing red warm-up jackets with "Big Red Machine" in white lettering. A wire-service feature on me that off-season by writer Ira Berkow talked again about me hustling on a walk—"he will run down first base as if it were a burglar"—and asked if I would burn myself out. "The answer is no, because Pete Rose is smart like a Phoenix. He rises afresh from the ashes of his sweat."

If that was true, it was all because of my dad. I sat down with Bob Hertzel of the *Enquirer* that off-season, and ended up talking to him about my dad, who was still catching the same afternoon bus every day to make it home on time from his job downtown at the bank. I played basketball with my dad the first week of December and to me he looked as fit as ever. The man was unstoppable.

"He's a rock," I told Bob. "He's fifty-eight years old. But to look at him, you'd swear he was only forty-four. He's not fat at all. He's got steel-gray hair. He stands five feet eleven. He weighs a hundred ninety pounds. He's a sharper dresser than I am. And even though he's a grandfather, he still hustles. He never walks when he can run."

I'd had the same haircut for years, partly because in those days the Reds had so many rules about not having long hair or facial hair or even long socks. That off-season I let my hair grow a little and went with a more mod cut, something longer and more stylish. Pictures of my new do ran in papers all over the country. Then they flew me out to California for a fancy Baseball Awards Dinner in Beverly Hills. People were doing double takes seeing the new Pete Rose.

"Now I know why you come to all these benefits," Casey Stengel commented. "So they can recognize your new face."

Back home afterward, that Wednesday I went over to Kentucky to get a haircut from my longtime barber, Harry. My sister Caryl knew where I was and called me at Harry's, which was very much out of the ordinary.

"Caryl, what is it?" I said.

"Dad died," she told me.

I was shocked.

"No, no, you mean Mom," I said, and I meant it. Dad? He was healthy as an ox. Mom had always had health problems.

"No," she said, "I mean Dad. Dad died."

It's nearly fifty years later as I write these words now. I'm a man pushing eighty soon enough, and I can tell you I'm still shocked, to this day, at the news I received from my sister. My dad was never sick in his whole life. He didn't even have a doctor. How could he have just died in his fifties?

The details, as I heard in the hours ahead, were typical of my dad. He'd been at his job at the bank and on his way out of the building when he started to feel some discomfort. Another man would have asked for help and had a doctor look at him, and maybe they'd have been able to help him. Not my dad. He didn't want to inconvenience anybody. So he got on the same bus he took every day, rode the forty-five-minute ride home. He walked up the hill to our house and saw my mother before he collapsed and died of a heart attack.

I was in a fog that whole month after he died. Maybe in a way my whole life since he died has been in a fog. A part of me died with him, I know that much. That was the first time I ever went through something like that. I remember going down to Vitt & Stermer Funeral Home to arrange for visitation hours that Friday from 4 P.M. to 9 P.M. and for the funeral services that Saturday morning.

The owner, John Stermer, came out to see me and asked if I had any questions. He probably meant about the arrangements or something like that, but I don't know what came over me. Like I said, it was the first time I'd ever been through anything like that, and I just started asking him questions, maybe to get my mind off what was going on.

"John, can I ask you a question?" I said. "If you get a body that comes in here and it's unrecognizable, you can't get a match from his fingerprints or his teeth, how do you estimate how old he is?"

Stermer, who inherited the business from his father, gave me a level look. He'd had more of these kinds of talks than I had, that was for sure.

"That's a good question," he said. "The way we do it is by examining the fluid in the body. It's not always accurate. Your father had the fluid of a forty-year-old man in his body. If he came in, unrecognizable, I would have told someone that he was a male, forty years old or so."

My dad had so many friends, from all the sports teams he'd played on, from the bank, from all kinds of different walks of life, and he'd died so young, so suddenly, the funeral that Saturday morning was packed. He had played football for so many years and had so many competitors who loved him, and the bank people loved him, too. There were a couple hundred people there, easy.

There was no way in the world I could speak or say anything. Just getting through the day was going to be a big enough challenge. I was surprised to find myself listening closely to what the pastor had to say. Usually my thoughts wander, but he had my full attention.

"The moment you're born, you start to die," he said at my father's funeral. "It's only a matter of time. Everybody's got a date."

I walked out of there afterward and those words were still with me, echoing. It was a weird deal. But you realize it's part of life.

There was an obituary in the *Cincinnati Enquirer* that paid proper respect to all my dad had done as an athlete and all he meant to the community. And it acknowledged all he had done for me.

"It was a love affair, a deep, warm, wonderful love affair, and now it's over," Bob Hertzel wrote in a separate article over on the sports page. "In a flash, a moment in time, it ended as Pete Rose Sr. breathed his last breath Wednesday. . . . Gone was the man who had made Pete Rose into the person he is . . . a personable, enthusiastic, friendly, dedicated, and ambitious human being. It was the end of a love affair between father and son and only young Pete Rose will ever know how close he was to his father and how thankful he was for the home and guidance that had been provided for him."

The holidays that year were not what you'd call festive. My dad's funeral was less than two weeks before Christmas. I had the rest of my family to think of, I had to be strong for all of them, but I was in deep shock. I felt lost. I felt hurt. I felt confused. My dad had always been my guiding light. I did everything for him. All I could think was "He died too young, he died too young."

Then I started to see it in a different way. I started to realize how lucky I was to have loved my dad the way I did and to have him love me the way he did. If you're really close to somebody and they die, you soon see that they're always going to be there with you. You don't ever lose that. I have so many good memories of my dad; I have no bad memories. If I ever want a smile on my face, I just think about all the good times when I watched him play, and watched him get on the bus to go to work or get off the bus after a day at work.

To this day, all these years later, I still miss my dad like crazy, but I'm not going to get teary-eyed. I miss him more than anybody, but he repaid me in every way, and maybe I kind of repaid him by working hard and making it to the big leagues. He went to spring training every year and loved it. He got to see me win Rookie of the Year. He got to see me win my first batting title on the last day of the season, and then win another one on the last day of the next season. He got to see me in the All-Star Game when I won the game after colliding with Ray Fosse. He got to see me in the World Series. So I repaid him a little bit. Not enough—I could never do that—but a little bit.

PART 4

LIFE AS BIG PETE

CHAPTER 20

Brawling at Shea

'd been in the top ten in voting for National League MVP six years in a row, from 1965 to 1970, including that second-place showing in 1968, but other players always got in the way. I'd always fallen short, until 1973, when I was finally named MVP of the league. Winning MVP honors was good personally, but to me MVP meant above all that I was really helping the team. You're not going to get voted MVP unless you're making your mark in a way that carried others along.

But you know what? It felt a little hollow, empty. I couldn't call my dad, like I always would, to tell him about it. He would have enjoyed it, but life had other ideas for me. With my dad gone, I was Big Pete now. All those years I'd been working, working, working to show him I could live up to the example he set. Now I could only show myself—and my teammates and the fans.

The Reds had a hard time living up to the promise of our 102-win, World Series team of 1970. The next season, we actually finished under .500, if you can believe it, winding up 79–83 and tied for fourth place in the National League West, with only one team behind us, the expansion San Diego Padres. I had another good year, but if the team isn't winning, who cares?

November 1971 brought bad news, as far as I was concerned. My buddy Tommy Helms had been traded away along with Lee "Who's Got It?" May, whose power hitting had carried us at times for years. Both were two-time All-Stars and Lee had been MVP of the Reds in '71. We also dealt backup Jimmy Stewart. So what did we get? A whole package of players, including outfielders Cesar Geronimo and Ed Armbrister, and we got Joe Morgan, a talented second baseman, to be sure, but then so was Tommy Helms. It made no sense to the fans, and even the press was skeptical.

I was curious how the trade would work out. I could see positives. Joe Morgan was a very smart ballplayer. The guys we were losing were tremendous teammates, but sometimes shuffling the deck worked out well. I liked Joe's speed and his toughness and I liked the idea of having him hit just behind me in the lineup. He had some pop and was a good situational hitter.

Here's what he said when he heard about the trade: "I think maybe I'll get to play in the World Series now."

We were all sure we were heading to the series together. In '72, with Joe in the lineup and Tony Perez back at first base, we won 95 games and beat the Pirates in a 5-game National League Championship Series. We took the Oakland A's to 7 games in the World Series and fell just short. That was the series where Gene Tenace came out of nowhere to explode for 4 home runs, and Catfish Hunter and Rollie Fingers anchored their pitching staff. We blew them out 8–1 in Game 6, and then in Game 7 lost by one run, 3–2.

To say we were hungry in 1973 would be an understatement. We'd been to the World Series two of the previous three years and lost both times. We knew we had a good enough team to win it all. We won 99 games to run away with the National League West, and went up against the New York Mets in the NLCS. We were a powerhouse, and they weren't even a good team. Most of the season, they'd been under .500, and then they won a few games late to finish 82–79. The rules back then were screwy. They scheduled the series before the season even started, and in this case that meant Game 5, if it came to that, would be in New York. Not that we cared. We figured we'd roll right over that team.

We won the first game at home, and then Jon Matlack shut us out in Game 2 to even up the series. That set up a day game at Shea Stadium that a lot of people figured would decide the series. We were already down 6–0 by the time I came up in the third inning for my second at bat. I singled as part of a two-run rally to make it a little closer. The mood at Shea was loud and ugly by the time I came up again in the fifth, the scoreboard showing the Mets up 9–2, but I knew how explosive our offense was. We were never out of it. I singled and then Joe Morgan, up next, bounced a tailor-made double-play ball to shortstop Bud Harrelson. I did what I always did: I went in hard to try to break up the double play. That was when all hell broke loose.

I had no problem with Buddy. He was a little guy and had to be tough. He was jawing with me, accusing me of a cheap shot, calling me names, and the next thing I knew Mets third baseman Wayne Garrett was jumping into the action and we had a full-scale brawl on our hands. Watching the game on TV back home, my three-year-old son, Pete Jr., had said: "Daddy fights just like Joe Frazier!" They call that one of the most famous baseball fights ever. The crowd at Shea was worked up into such a bloodlust, they were about ready to riot.

Back out in left field to play defense, I was being pelted with just about everything you could imagine, from apples to tin cans to batteries. Then some guy threw an empty bottle of Jack Daniel's whiskey at me from the third deck—you know, one of those thick-glass bottles—and it missed me by two or three feet.

I called time out and walked in to talk to my manager, Sparky Anderson.

"Spark, they just threw a whiskey bottle out," I told him.

"That's enough for us today," he said. "Let's go."

And we walked off the field. It was a joke. No one could be expected to play under those conditions. It was like being a Roman gladiator or something.

Chub Feeney, the National League president, went down on the field to huddle with the umpires, and they sent out a delegation of Mets to the outfield to try to calm that mob down. You had Willie Mays out there, his last season in the big leagues, pleading with the fans, and it was touch and go whether we could even play on. Finally we did.

That crowd was so full of hate for me, I was warned not to go out to dinner in New York after the game. Can you imagine? I was Public Enemy No. 1 in New York at the time.

Game 4 back at Shea went into extra innings, tied 1–1. We loaded up the bases in the tenth and Tony Perez flied to right to end the threat. Then in the twelfth I came up against Harry Walker, who'd just come into the game, with one out. The Shea Stadium fans were all over me. There were crude signs all over the place in the outfield, reading things like ROSE IS A WEED and HEY ROSE WE DON'T FORGET, letting me know how they felt about me. I shut them up by hitting a home run to right, and we won 2–1.

"They hated his guts, those people in Shea," Chub Feeney said later, "but when he hit it, I'd say 70 percent of those Mets fans stood up and cheered him. He makes you like him."

Well, maybe, but out in the outfield for the deciding Game 5, I was still getting pelted. It was crazy. We were the best team in the league and because of the rules back then, we had to play three games in a row at Shea. It was bad enough having to go against Tom Seaver and Tug McGraw; we were going against a whole city that had lost its mind. I doubled and scored in the top of the fifth to tie it up 2–2, but the Mets answered right away with four runs, and by the time I came up in the top of the ninth, we were down 7–2. I walked, and ran to first base—of course I did!—and was out there when Dan Driessen grounded out to end the thing and the fans rushed the field, blood in their eyes.

I was thinking to myself: We're in America, playing baseball for the right to go to the World Series, and those fans were so unruly it was total chaos. I wasn't playing against the New York Mets in that series, I was playing against the whole damn city of New York. That was the only time in my life I was ever scared in a baseball uniform. I made it halfway to second base on Driessen's grounder. I saw fans out on the field converging on me from every direction and just put my head down and ran for the dugout. It was like I was back in high school, showing my broken-field running moves as a swivel-hipped halfback, just making it through that crowd. I'll never forget it: I looked up and saw six or seven of my teammates standing up on the top step of the dugout, each of them with a bat in his hands, ready to swing.

"Our first concern was Pete's safety," Johnny Bench told reporters after we'd all retreated. "I thought someone might try to kill him. If the cops weren't going to stop those maniacs, then we would."

We lost the game, but the riot that broke out afterward meant everyone lost. "New York doesn't deserve a pennant," I said afterward. "They let the fans out of the zoo for the ball game and take them back when it's over."

I'd had a good series, leading us in hits with 8 and a .381 average—for those looking back through the lens of today's baseball talk, a 1.149 OPS—and none of it mattered. I'd led the league in hits (230) and average (.338), and added 64 RBIs, but none of that mattered either. It was a tough loss to swallow.

In November, when the postseason awards were announced, I was still a little out of joint about our having lost to the Mets the way we had. I hoped I wouldn't be disappointed again.

I was sitting at home at about 7 P.M. when the phone rang. "Congratulations," Jack Lang told me. "You have won the National League's Most Valuable Player award."

I always cared more about winning than anything else. That meant playing harder than anyone and it also meant trying to be a great teammate who made everyone around him better. That to me was what it was all about. It wasn't selfless or selfish, it was who I was, at the core. I cared about every one of my teammates and always tried to think of what might help them and what might get them going. If my style of play rubbed off on others, nothing made me happier. Now I was being recognized for both my play and my leadership, finishing ahead of the Pirates' Willie Stargell in voting by a panel of sportswriters.

"A year ago Pete Rose was a good baseball player," the *Cincinnati Enquirer* wrote. "He was a good player two, three, four years ago. But greatness waited until 1973 before it entered his life. It had not to do with his performance on the field. It had to do, instead, with his performance off the field. Maturity struck the man and the result was that he became a team leader; an inspiration at a time when inspiration is needed, not only on the baseball field but in the American way of life."

I'd have loved for my dad to be around to read those words in the paper, but even more so I wished he could have heard the tribute from Joe Morgan, a great teammate and great leader himself.

"It's contagious, the way he goes out and hustles every day," Joe told reporters. "It rubs off. With things going bad at the start of the season and with the kids we had, we needed leadership. We were looking for someone to pull us out of it and he was the man. I can't think of anyone who you could follow every day like Rose."

CHAPTER 21

Some Kind of Game

I was leading the Reds in hitting during the 1975 season when Sparky called me into his office to talk.

"Petey, we've got to add more offense to the team," he told me.

"What the hell do you want me to do?" I said. "I'm leading the league in hitting."

He smiled at that.

"Move to third base," he said.

One more time, I was changing positions, and I was happy to do it for the good of the team.

The next day, George Sugar, one of Sparky's coaches, hit ground balls to me at third base for three hours. There were a few glitches as I got used to playing third, but soon we got past them—and we added George Foster's bat. We were by then a good enough team to expect to be playing in the postseason, but we'd have to earn it.

I was lucky to have played in the greatest World Series ever, let alone having starred in it. I'm talking of course about the 1975 series between the Boston Red Sox and my Reds. For my money, it was

the greatest ever, and plenty of people agree with me. I'll never forget
coming up in the top of the tenth inning of Game 6 of that series at
Fenway Park in Boston, and turning to look at the Red Sox catcher,
Carlton Fisk.

"Say, this is some kind of game, isn't it?" I said.

Two innings later it was after midnight, 12:34 A.M. to be exact,
when Carlton came up and hit the most famous 304-foot home run
in the history of baseball. I was playing third base and as the ball sailed
over my head, I didn't think it was gone. I watched it float down the
line. The last thing I was doing was watching Fisk, but everyone who
watched at home remembers what they saw on NBC.

Here's how Roger Angell summed it up: "Fisk waving wildly,
weaving and writhing and gyrating along the first-base line, as he
wished the ball fair, *forced* it fair with his entire body. He circled the
bases in triumph, in sudden company with several hundred fans, and
jumped on home plate with both feet, and John Kiley, the Fenway
Park organist, played Handel's 'Hallelujah Chorus,' *fortissimo.*"

It was dramatic all right. Just don't ask me what *fortissimo* means.
Sounds good, though. The game had already featured a three-run
homer in the first by Fred Lynn, a rookie out of California who'd had
a great year for Boston and would earn both Rookie of the Year and
MVP honors that season; a home run from our center fielder, Cesar
Geronimo, part of our building a 6–3 lead; and then in the bottom
of the eighth, a three-run home run by Bernie Carbo to tie it up.
Carbo yelled out to me as he ran the base paths, saying didn't I wish
I was that strong, and I just laughed it off. The Red Sox loaded the
bases in the ninth with no outs and George Foster made a bang-bang

play, catching a fly from Fred Lynn and throwing Denny Doyle out at the plate. I'm not sure I'd have been able to make the same play if it had been me in left field. Joe Morgan looked to have won the game with a deep drive to right field, but Dwight Evans made a great catch near the visitors' bullpen to rob him. Then came the Fisk homer and all of New England celebrating and turning poetic about what a beautiful game it was, except for one small thing: We still had a Game 7 to play.

We had a hell of a team that year. Sparky had asked me to move from left field to third so we could add George Foster, and I was happy to make the move, which gave us one more dangerous bat. We clinched first place on September 7, a record, and went on to win 108 games in the regular season. We swept the Pirates in the NLCS, blowing them out in the first two games at home and then winning in extras in Game 3. That to us was the hard part. The playoffs were more pressure in those days, and I'll tell you why: You're playing against guys you played against all summer, and it's a quick series, just three of five, so if you blinked, you were heading home. Nowadays it's four out of seven for the NLCS and ALCS, so you can afford to fuck up one game.

I never did think there was any pressure playing in the World Series. Sure, every single guy playing wants to win, but for me it was just such a pleasure to be there. You've made it to the ultimate showcase for baseball that year, you're in the thick of the action, and if you don't love that, why are you playing the game? I always played as hard as I could, so I didn't have to think about turning it up a notch or anything like that. You're so into it as a player, but at the same time, you're enjoying the twists and turns the same way the fan at home does, and that 1975 World Series had enough twists and turns for a dozen or two postseasons.

Boston won the first game by a lot, and then we took the next two games by one run after a lot of lead changes. Then it was the Red Sox's turn to win a one-run game, evening the series up at two games apiece, and we rolled to a 6–2 win at home in Game 5, led by Big Dog, who had two home runs in the game. I added an RBI double. We flew back to Boston knowing we just had to win one game. Rain pushed Game 6 back, and the writers had to find something to write about.

"Pete is what baseball's all about," Jim Murray wrote in the *Los Angeles Times*. "Pete is the kind of guy who would lead cheers if he couldn't make the team. Pete is the kind of guy who would say, 'Take me, sir,' in a suicide mission. . . . Pete was born running and he goes through life as if he were skipping rope. Or as if the world were stairs he was taking two at a time. He's got the face of a small boy looking in a candy store window. He plays the game as if it was one o'cat on an empty lot with the pure joy of a little kid with his cap turned backwards and one black tooth or eye."

We were back at Fenway Park for Game 7 the next day after Fisk's game-winning home run, and for us it was all water under the bridge. We just had to win one game and were sure that's what we were going to do. Even when our starter Don Gullett lost his control and walked in two runs in the third to make it a 3–0 Boston lead, we were all sure we were going to get to Red Sox starter Bill Lee, the Spaceman, sooner or later. They didn't call him the Spaceman for nothing.

I led off the sixth inning with a sharp single to left and then Joe Morgan flied out to right. Johnny Bench, up next, bounced what looked like a double-play ball to short, except I was never going to let them turn two and get out of the inning. I slid so hard into their second basemen, Denny Doyle, I knocked him on his ass and he threw the ball into the Boston dugout, so no inning-ending double play. The next pitch, Bill Lee threw Tony Perez an Eephus pitch, one of those big looping lobs, and Tony blasted it over the Jimmy Fund sign in left field for a two-run homer. The moral of that story is, if I don't break that play up and they get out of the inning, they probably win the World Series, because it's 3–0 and we have no momentum. After that we had all the confidence in the world. With that team you knew someone was going to hit a home run in a crucial situation.

My next time up, I singled home Ken Griffey to tie it up, and in the ninth I walked and was on base when Joe Morgan singled home the go-ahead run. Three outs later, we were world champions—and as I was getting doused with champagne and beer in the visitors' clubhouse, they told me I was MVP of the series. I thought of my dad and all the great fans back home in Cincinnati and just let the emotion of it roll all over me.

When you get to hold the trophy up for the first time as a world champion, it's a feeling you can never get again. It's indescribable. You worked so hard for this moment your whole life, and all of a sudden you hold the trophy up. I don't think guys who cover the game or watch the game on TV know what it feels like to win as a player or as a manager. You have to live it to understand it. As an athlete, it's the kind of feeling that once you get it, you want it every year. Every fricking year, you want to have that feeling again, because it means so much.

Winning that World Series meant everything to Johnny. It meant everything to Joe. It meant everything to Big Dog and Davey. But I have to believe it meant even more to me, because I was a Cincinnati kid. I was born there. All the years I played with those guys, I was playing for the people of Cincinnati, because they were my people. That's why it meant even more to me. If we'd been playing a World Series in Binger, Oklahoma, that would have meant even more to Johnny. Or Oakland for Joe. Or Cuba for Tony. It means more to you if those are your people.

"I feel happier for the people of Cincinnati and our area than I do myself," I told reporters. "There will be twenty-five thousand people in Fountain Square for a celebration tomorrow and I know twenty thousand of them. After all, I grew up in Cincinnati. I'm getting chills right now thinking about it. It's a great feeling, a feeling I've never had before."

We won two World Series in a row with that team, but it was that first one that would always stand out. A year later, we had the same team back. We didn't lose anybody to free agency and we didn't make any changes. We won 102 games and finished ten games ahead of the Dodgers in the National League West, then swept the Pirates in the NLCS and swept the Yankees in the World Series. We won every game, seven out of seven.

For me as a player, the '76 World Series was boring. The year before, five of our seven World Series games were tight, one-run games. This year, only one of four was. We won each of the other three games by four runs or more. It was also cold. You were glad you won. You were glad you had swept the Yankees. But sweeping the World Series was like winning the Super Bowl 55–0. It was not good for your sport.

The only thing I enjoyed about the '76 World Series (besides winning, of course) was playing against Thurman Munson, a quality player and a quality person, who was named captain of that Yankees team, the first Yankees team captain since Lou Gehrig. Munson would have been a Hall of Famer, no question, but he died three years later when he crashed his Cessna Citation plane.

It was really fun to play against Thurman. He was a player's player, always playing hard but having fun and ready to talk. Graig Nettles and Chris Chambliss were good players, but they didn't talk much. Lou Piniella was a great talker, but he was out in left field. Thurman was right behind home plate, ready to trade wisecracks with you. He had that quality of the great ones that he was so focused, so into the game, he could be totally relaxed. You knew that nothing out there scared him.

He'd have been a great Red, but we didn't have any room for him. I was playing with the greatest catcher of all time, Johnny Bench. Thurman was better with a bat, more of a .300 hitter, but no way was he close to being the receiver that Johnny Bench was. They were the offensive stars of that series. Munson batted .529, Bench .533. But we were a complete team, top to bottom, businesslike and efficient.

"A helluva team," said Joe DiMaggio afterward. "They do everything. They hit the ball. They run. They are tough on the field. From the top of the order to the bottom, they can hurt you."

CHAPTER 22

Winning with the Phillies

I would have been glad to play my entire career for my hometown team if the Reds' brass had given me a chance to do that. All I'd ever wanted was to be a Red. But by the start of the 1979 season, I was going to be thirty-eight years old, and I knew sooner or later I'd start hearing talk about how I was slowing down. Now, if they'd have talked to Uncle Buddy or anyone in Cincinnati with a memory, they'd have known my dad was starring on the football field for the old Cincinnati Bengals into his forties. They'd have remembered that men in my family, besides maturing late, aged slower. I was a long ways from slowing down—in '78 I'd had a record forty-four-game hitting streak—but I was starting to wonder if the Reds really wanted me back for a seventeenth season.

Joe DiMaggio was always one of my favorite players, so making a run at his record fifty-six-game hitting streak that summer was a huge thrill for me. Word kind of got out once I ran my streak to thirty games, and all of a sudden I had a lot more reporters to talk to every day. I didn't mind. I always went out of my way to try to give the guys—it was always guys, back then—something to put in their newspapers or magazines or to talk about on radio. Everyone thought the streak had ended that July 19 when I walked in the eighth against the Phillies and still didn't have a hit. Would you believe it? My guys batted around in the ninth, I came up again—and dropped down a bunt base hit to run the streak to thirty-two. I tied Wee Willie Keeler's 1897 record of forty-four straight games, but that was as far as I got. I was happy to bring a few more thrills for my home-town fans.

In October 1978, I declared my free agency and gave a list of teams I'd be interested in hearing offers from, including the Reds, of course, as well as the Phillies, Padres, and Dodgers in the NL and five teams in the AL, including the Red Sox and Yankees. The announcement led to a lot of quotes from baseball people saying they all wished I'd stay in Cincinnati. The *Chicago Tribune* ran a column, CINCINNATI WITHOUT ROSE LIKE PARIS WITHOUT TOWER, that began, "Imagine . . . the Eiffel Tower picking up and trucking off to Bonn because it felt unloved in Paris. . . . Pete Rose, Cincinnati's human monument, its sturdiest, most admirable edifice, is about to pick up and leave. Pete Rose is going to be a free agent."

How things have changed! That was the third year of free agency in baseball, and back then it was considered almost scandalous to declare yourself a free agent. I'd agreed to go on a tour of Japan with a group of Reds players after the '78 season, and I almost didn't go. We were on the plane flying to Japan and had a stopover in Anchorage, Alaska, to gas up. I hadn't enjoyed the flight at all. With my coming free agency, things had soured. I got off the plane and went to look for a payphone to call my longtime agent, Reuven Katz.

"Reuven," I said. "These guys are treating me like a piece of shit. Should I just come home?" That was what I wanted to do.

"No, you can't come home," Reuven told me. "You've got too many appearances over there and your picture is on every ticket. That wouldn't look good to back out now."

So I gutted it out. We had seventeen exhibition games scheduled. I got back on the plane in Anchorage and flew to Tokyo and showed up with the rest of the guys when we went to Korakuen Stadium for a practice and session with the press. I turned down an offer to play for the Seibu Lions for more than a million dollars.

"Yes, I'll play in Japan," I said, adding, "seventeen games."

While I was still in Japan, twelve teams came out as formally interested in landing my services. We'd started slow over there, and then won the next twelve to finish 14–2–1. The Japanese fans loved me. I was busting my ass, diving for everything in the outfield, making headfirst slides, doing everything the way I always did it, but over there this was new. I went hitless in the last game, against the Yomiuri Giants and Sadaharu Oh, the legendary Japanese slugger, or I'd have had a seventeen-game hitting streak. The Japanese took a liking to me because I gave them their money's worth.

Once we got back to Cincinnati, I got together with the Reds' coaching staff and some others who had helped me and gave them each a token of my appreciation. I'd asked them all what color Jeep they wanted. When we got back from Japan, we had a lunch at the Holiday Inn, and I had nine Jeeps parked out front. I gave every coach a Jeep. I had the names on a piece of cardboard in every window. Larry Shepard, our pitching coach, was from Lincoln, Nebraska, and wanted a snowplow on the front of his Jeep, so I even got him a snowplow. I paid $50,000 for ten of them and kept one for myself, I liked them so much. I even gave one to our equipment manager, Bernie Stowe, and our broadcaster, Joe Nuxhall, who used to throw batting practice for me when no one else would.

One of the first cities I visited to pick my new team was Atlanta, and team owner Ted Turner picked me up at the airport. He was driving a Toyota. You had to get a kick out of that. This guy won the America's Cup yacht race, and here he was, behind the wheel of a Toyota. Ted was very keen. His SuperStation TBS had just been created that year, and he needed programming—like, me sliding head-first into second base in a Braves uniform every game. He offered me a million a year for four years. I remember I used to have a little eight-minute tape of highlights of me playing that I showed all the guys, and I started to show Ted Turner.

"Listen, I don't need to see a tape on how Pete Rose plays base-ball," he said. "I know how he plays baseball. I want him to help me sell TV."

When I went to St. Louis and negotiated with Augie Busch, he'd had a hernia operation and was in the hospital. If I knew then what I know now, I'd have signed with the Cardinals. They even offered me a Budweiser distributorship—that would have been a nice thing to fall back on. But they wanted me to replace Lou Brock and I wasn't interested in doing that.

The Pirates were also interested, and I met with their owner, John Galbreath, at his Darby Dan Farm in Lexington, Kentucky. He offered me racehorses. He had a beautiful horse, Roberto, named after Clemente. He knew how much I loved horses, but I didn't think I could make Pittsburgh a winner.

Another guy who made a tempting offer was Ewing Kauffman of Kansas City. "You know something, Pete," he said. "You come over here and you can beat that hits record, because you can be a designated hitter. I know your dad played football until he was forty-two years old."

Ewing had done his homework.

"Mr. Kauffman, I really appreciate the kind words and your thoughtfulness and your being willing to offer me a contract," I said, "but at this stage of my career, being thirty-eight, I'm not really interested in changing leagues, because if I change leagues I have to redo all the pitchers in the league that are in my head. Based on that, I'm going to pass."

"I appreciate that," he said. "If you change your mind, just get back to us." And he offered me an already proven oil well.

Ted Turner called back after I'd met with several other teams. "I already offered a million a year for four years," he told Reuven. "Tell Pete I'll give him $100,000 every year of his life after he retires until he dies, plus the $4 million."

That was an incredible offer. But at that time, I thought the Braves were a long ways off from being winners. I wanted to go to Philadelphia because they had great players like Larry Bowa, Mike Schmidt, and Greg Luzinski. Everyone was assuming I'd be signing with the Phils. I went to Philadelphia and went out to owner Ruly Carpenter's house. I'd just come off of reaching my three thousandth hit in 1978 and I had hit in forty-four straight games. I told Mr.

Carpenter I wanted to be the highest-paid player in sports, so Reuven asked him for $810,000.

"My god, that's almost a million dollars," Carpenter said.

We thought we were dead, because that was just too much money for him. I had a press conference at Veterans Stadium to announce it was a no-go. The papers quoted Carpenter saying, "There's a limit beyond which the Phillies cannot go."

But as we were riding back to the airport with Bill Giles, who ran the business part of the team, he turned to Reuven. "I have an idea," he said. "I'll get back to you in a couple days."

I had no idea what he was talking about. He called back a couple days later to say that he'd lined up sponsors so they could come up on salary. There was one problem the Phillies had in the '70s. You know what it was? Me. I was always tough on them. If I left the Reds, they didn't have that problem.

I already had better offers from Atlanta, Kansas City, and St. Louis, but I went with Philadelphia and signed for $810,000 a year. I already got along with Schmidt and Luzinski—I'd been going out with them for dinner from time to time.

Change was good for me. I knew that I had to start all over in a lot of ways. It didn't matter how many games I'd played or how many hits I'd collected by then, I was a new face on that team. I didn't walk in for spring training in '79 with the Phillies and announce, "Hey, I'm your team leader, let's get going." It wasn't that way. We laid the groundwork my first season for what was to come later. I didn't ask for respect. I played like I thought I deserved it and let the rest take care of itself. I waited for that process to unfold naturally over my first season in Philly, and batted .331 that season with 208 hits. After my new teammates saw me play for a year and knew I wasn't a phony-baloney, then I could expect to be heard.

One time we were playing in New York and I got served with divorce papers. I went 22 for 30 over the coming games.

"How the hell do you do it?" Greg Luzinski asked me. "How do you get hot like that when you've just been served divorce papers?"

"Greg," I said, "I knew I was going to get divorced. Am I better off if I hit .340 or hit .140?"

He got the idea.

"I never let anything at home affect me," I said. "I never take that out onto the field. If you let it bother you as a player, you're affecting the other guys on the team."

When I joined the Phillies for the '79 season, Mike Schmidt was the best player in the game three or four days a week. He could be more than that, and when he watched me play over the course of a season, Mike became the best player in the game seven days a week. I spurred him on. I made him understand that there are other ways to win than home runs. You can lead with your defense. You can lead with your base-running. You can lead with your leadership.

"Mike, you're the best player in baseball," I told him. "You can't hit a home run every day, but you've got to go out and play like the best player in baseball every day."

Mike had an MVP season in 1980, finishing the regular season with forty-eight homers and 121 RBIs. I led the Phillies that season in hits with 185 and doubles with forty-two, showing that I might be thirty-nine years old, but I could still leg out a double. That club had a ton of talent before I showed up, Schmidt and Luzinski and second baseman Manny Trillo and Larry Bowa at short, and center fielder Garry Maddox and Bake McBride in right. The pitching staff was anchored by Cy Young winner Steve Carlton. They were almost there, but not quite.

I'd promised the organization that if they signed me, we would make that last step and go to the World Series, and I delivered. I made everyone else play harder. By the time we showed up for Game 1 of the series that year at Veterans Stadium in Philadelphia, squaring off against the Kansas City Royals, the sportswriters were cranking it up, talking about my sparkplug effect on the team. That was a different era, I tell you. The writers used to let it fly a whole lot more.

"If he has to crash into the catcher to score the winning run, then he'll do it," Art Spander wrote in the *San Francisco Examiner* that October. "That's the way Pete Rose plays. That's the way he's always played. Baseball isn't a game to Pete Rose, it's an obsession. He goes after it like a missionary goes after pagans."

To my point about how little things help win games, we broke open Game 1 of that series with a five-run rally in the third inning. My contribution? I was hit by a pitch that grazed off my leg, and then I came around to score on Bake McBride's home run. Their starter, Dennis Leonard, had been tough on me. I was looking to help my team. I never purposely got hit by a pitch—well, except maybe one time against Phil Niekro, a knuckle-baller—but then again, I wasn't scared to get hit by the ball. I got hit 110 times in my career. We held on to win 7–6, and won again the next game, but the Royals pulled off an extra-inning win for Game 3 and then cruised in Game 4 to even it up. Up until Game 6, every game in the series had been close,

a one-run or two-run contest, but we closed it out with a 4–1 excla-
mation point of a win in front of 65,838 roaring fans at Veterans
Stadium. That last game was watched on television by 54.9 million
viewers, which still stands as the record.

For all the talent we had on that team, for all the great chemistry
and competitiveness you felt every time you walked in that clubhouse, I still feel to this day that the reason we won it all that year
was because our manager, Dallas Green, was the perfect fit for that
team. Mike Schmidt may have been the best player in the game at
that moment, Luzinski was a four-time All-Star, and Gary Maddox
was called the Secretary of Defense for good reason. But we won
that year because of Dallas Green. He came in and he was the kind
of manager we needed, a kick-ass-type manager who didn't take no
shit from nobody. He was vocal and no nonsense; he had rules and
he wanted you to abide by the rules. If you didn't, he penalized you.
He didn't let anybody slide with anything, whether it was Mike
Schmidt or me or the rawest rookie—we all had the same rules. He
cracked the whip and got everyone's attention.

I wasn't playing for my hometown fans anymore, but I was playing for history. The people of Philadelphia had to wait fifty years for
a World Series championship. That's how long it had been since a
Philadelphia team—the Athletics, in 1930, led by Lefty Grove—had
won the World Series. I remember when I went back to Philly during
the off-season after that series. Every time I walked down a street
somewhere in town, people would stop me and tell me, "Thanks."
The World Series always means a lot, but when you wait fifty years,
that makes it that much more special, like when the Red Sox and
Cubs finally won it after keeping their fans waiting so long. It was a

good feeling to know I'd helped make so many people happy. And it was a good feeling to know the fans of Philadelphia had embraced me. I'd switched teams and won another World Series, my third. Six months before my fortieth birthday, I was still playing the game the way my dad taught me to play it, all out all the time.

CHAPTER 23

A Big League Skipper

During my years playing for Sparky Anderson, I would go down to the end of the dugout whenever I could and sit there eating sunflower seeds. I wanted to be as close as I could to Sparky so I could pepper him with questions. It drove him nuts, but I was always thinking along with him, and the questions just kept coming. I played for twelve managers and Sparky was the best of all of them. He was just street smart. He didn't go to college. Sparky was a street guy. I was a street guy. I didn't have no education. My education was sports. I'd be the last guy to win a spelling bee.

Sparky had two great rules, which I used myself when I became a manager. One was no wives or girlfriends go to the playoffs. The playoffs are all business. The other rule was no kids in the clubhouse after a game at home if we lost. That's a great rule, because every kid who went to the game every night, and we had a lot of them, would sit there hoping their dads would win so they could go in the clubhouse after the game. It might not sound that important, but you had to think these things through ahead of time to help set the tone you wanted for your club.

Sparky ended up managing the Reds for nine seasons, and then moved to the American League, where he managed the Detroit Tigers for seventeen years. He finished with a lifetime win-loss managing record of 2,194–1,834 and ranks sixth all-time in wins by a manager, behind only Connie Mack, John McGraw, Tony La Russa, Bobby Cox, and Joe Torre. His last season in Cincinnati was also my last season with the Reds, so we moved on together.

Dallas Green took over as the Phillies' skipper at the start of September during my first season in Philadelphia. One thing about Dallas: You always knew what you were getting with him. When he got hired, Dallas told reporters, "I express my thoughts. I'm a screamer, a yeller, and a cusser. I never hold back." No he didn't, and I liked it that way. I'd been known for years as a pretty fair screamer, yeller, and cusser myself. Dallas had his beefs with players, clashing with some, but he'd been minor league director and knew the personalities.

Dallas was an intelligent guy and pitched for the University of Delaware before the Phillies signed him. Other than Bake McBride, Manny Trillo, and me, all the key players on that team had come up through the Philly organization and Dallas had learned their quirks. He knew how to handle Bowa differently than Schmidt, and Schmidt differently than Maddox, and Maddox differently than Luzinski. If you know how to handle somebody, you have a better shot at getting the most out of them; it's just common sense.

I had five good seasons with the Phillies, but my last year in Philadelphia, it felt like time for a change. We had a good team again, winning ninety games and finishing in first place in the National

League East, but my average slipped to .245 on 121 hits and fifty-two runs scored, not Pete Rose–type numbers. I'd be turning forty-three the next spring, and at that age you can count on hearing talk about your bat speed declining, unless you continue to put up very strong numbers. I wasn't doing that.

Despite all that, I knew I was a good deal. I was only ten hits shy of four thousand, and when I reached that threshold, I'd be in striking distance of Ty Cobb's all-time record of 4,189 career hits, a record that a lot of smart baseball people thought no one would ever touch. Someone would be willing to take a chance on me, and in the end it was the Montreal Expos. That April, wearing the new uniform, I showed up at Riverfront Stadium with the visiting team, in search of my four thousandth hit. I only needed one. It would have been perfect. But the Reds pitchers didn't want to let me hit. The fans at Riverfront Stadium gave me a standing ovation when I came up the first time, and then went quiet every time a pitch was thrown to me, but they didn't have much to watch. I was walked four times, the only time in my entire career I was ever walked four times in one game. That cost me a chance of reaching the milestone in my hometown.

It was kind of funny. When I got my three thousandth hit in May 1978, I was with the Reds and I got it against Steve Rogers of the Expos, and the Montreal first baseman was one of my best friends, Tony Perez. If I'd have had one hit that day, I'd have been standing on first base wearing an Expos uniform and the first baseman would have been Big Dog, who was now back in a Reds uniform again. No such luck.

I hit number four thousand against the Phillies. My first time up, I hit a double down the right-field line off Jerry Koosman. That was baseball history, doing something that had been done only one other time in the history of the game, by Ty Cobb, but the only guy to come out to second base was Billy DeMars, the Expos' hitting coach. None of my new teammates came out. I got on good with Gary Carter and Tim Raines and Doug Flynn, but they all kind of stayed in the dugout. I gave the four thousandth hit ball to Billy DeMars as a thank-you.

I hurt my shoulder, which was cutting down on my playing time, and the Reds were struggling that season under manager Vern Rapp with the second-worst record in the National League. Dick Howsam, the Reds' president, thought they needed a change of manager and thought I'd be a great choice. He reached out to my attorney to relay his interest, but he wanted me back only as a manager. I said no. I still wanted to play. We started holding secret talks with them about the idea of returning to the Reds as a player-manager. They needed persuading on the player part. The more the team lost under Vern Rapp, the stronger my argument became.

Finally, when the Expos were in San Francisco playing the Giants that August, the deal came together and was announced. At the time I rejoined the Reds, via a trade for a minor leaguer, they were 50–70.

"He'll primarily be a manager with some pinch hitting and playing in an occasional game," Jim Ferguson, a Reds' spokesman, announced in confirming the move.

That wasn't quite how I saw it, but close enough. And anyway, I'd be the manager, filling out the lineup card—and for my first game back in a Reds' uniform, of course I penciled in myself at first base. I went 2 for 4 and drove in two runs, and we beat the Cubs 6–4 in front of the second-largest crowd of the season at Riverfront Stadium, behind Opening Day.

REDS WIN AMID "SERIES" ATMOSPHERE was the headline in the *Cincinnati Enquirer.*

"I got goose bumps all over my body," Dave Concepcion said.

"It was like electricity in the air," Dave Parker said.

"Not even a World Series would have created this kind of excitement," said Reds' president Bob Howsam.

Being a player-manager is more challenging than it might sound. I had to be real careful when I was playing first base. When I would go in to give the ball to the pitcher, if I went in too far, it counted as a visit to the mound. The umpire came out one time and said, "That's one, one visit." And I didn't have anyone warmed up in the bullpen at the time.

At one time in baseball, it was very common to have a lot of player-managers, but I was the last of the breed. Since my run as player-manager of the Reds, there has not been one player-manager in baseball. I don't know why that is. Both Frank Robinson and Joe Torre started out as player-managers. Ty Cobb and Tris Speaker were both player-managers. I could see how Ty might be a little challenging to play for, though, come to think of it.

"He was very tough to play for," Hall of Famer Charlie Gehringer told reporters years later. "Very demanding. He was so great himself that he couldn't understand why, if he told players how to do certain things, they couldn't do it as well as he did."

That was something you always had to watch as a manager who also could still play the game. I developed my own style as a manager. Sparky was known as Captain Hook because he would take pitchers out real quick. I wasn't like that. I'd look over to George Scherger, a coach for the Reds for many years and a great baseball man who had been a mentor to Sparky.

"Get 'em out of there!" George would always be saying.

I was more deliberate about making a change. Our most important player might have been Dave Parker. Dave Parker should be in the Hall of Fame. He was a batting champion, an MVP, a Golden Glover, a world champion. He was also a great teammate, and he and I were close. He was like my assistant and kept others in line. Dave kept an eye on the young players for me and helped them develop.

I didn't ask him to do it. He believed in Eric Davis, he believed in Eddie Milner, he believed in Gary Redus. They were all good players, but they were young. And you had a guy like Dave Parker, and they were going to listen to him. He was like me in a lot of ways: He was punctual, he played his ass off, he played every day, and he was from Cincinnati.

I loved managing because it was all about paying close attention to everything that happened on the field, and paying close attention to every single one of your players, and those were two things I did naturally anyway. It would be tough to manage in today's game, the way the front office ties your hands on so many things nowadays, but if someone declared me eligible again for a job in baseball, and the Reds or some other team wanted me back, I'd jump at the chance. Just don't think I'd let anyone fill out a lineup card for me—that's a manager's job.

CHAPTER 24

Hit King

We closed out the 1984 season at home against the Astros, and once again Rose the manager decided on Rose the first baseman to start and bat second in the lineup behind Dave Concepcion. It was only my twenty-sixth game of the season for the Reds as a player, and at that point I had thirty-two hits since coming home to Cincinnati. That Sunday I drove in three runs and went 3 for 5, helping us to a 7–6 win on Eddie Milner's sacrifice fly in the bottom of the ninth that ended the season on a positive note for the fans.

My second-inning double was the 726th of my career, moving me just past Stan Musial for the National League doubles record, but the record on my mind was Ty Cobb's. My three-hit day had pulled me to ninety-four hits shy of 4,191. For most of my time with the Reds, it would have taken me less than half a season to account for ninety-four hits. Now, as a player-manager seeing limited duty, it was going to take me longer, but I was sure I could reach my last major goal sometime the following season. I'd collected 100 or more hits for a record twenty-two straight seasons. But why did I have to wait so long for that season to roll around?

"It's a shame spring training doesn't start tonight," I said after the game.

As a manager I was 19–22 for my part of the season, an improvement on Vern Rapp's 50–70 mark, but not nearly enough of one. I liked managing. I felt like I'd spent my whole life preparing for the challenge. We were 14–9 in games when I'd started myself, and I'd batted .365 for the Reds.

Two days after the season ended, my second wife, Carol, gave birth to our first child together, a boy we named Tyler Edward Rose, but to us he was always Ty. A street near my old high school, Western Hills, was renamed Pete Rose Drive. All I could think about was getting started with the next season and starting to grind out hits. Come April, papers were running little boxes with updates on the Cobb-Rose Countdown or Career Hit Leaders charts showing the top sixteen, all the way down to Roberto Clemente (3,000) and Rod Carew (2,956). By early August I was within twenty-five hits and the media focused on me so much, they had to start making fun of all the attention.

"Reaching grocery shelves across the nation will be some 12 million boxes of Wheaties with a picture on the front of the boyishly keen face and pertinacious swing of forty-four-year-old Rose, hustler nonpareil, hitter nonpareil, and eternal kid nonpareil," Ira Berkow wrote in *The New York Times*. "On television commercials for Wheaties, film clips depict Rose through his career, rapping out one of his 4,000-plus hits; diving headfirst into second base with hardly a hint of the grace of Greg Louganis and surfacing safe—which was the whole idea anyway—with a white uniform black with dirt from neck to knees; scaling an outfield fence to pick off a drive, and running, running, running."

By September 1, I was six hits back from Cobb and, more important overall, Mike Schmidt and the Phillies had just pulled off a four-game sweep of the NL West–leading Dodgers in LA, meaning we were only six-and-a-half games out of first place. Like other guys chasing big records, I was spending hours talking to the media. That part of baseball had always come easy to me, and most of the time I liked it just fine, but they were getting sick of me and I was getting sick of them.

On September 11, at home, I came up in the first inning against Padres starter Eric Show and worked the count to 2–1. Show threw me an inside slider and I hit it to left-center field for a single. That was it. I had passed Ty Cobb's record, which had stood since 1928. The feeling was incredible.

"Thanks for the memories," the Padre first baseman Steve Garvey told me as I reached the bag.

Tommy Helms, my roommate and old friend through the minor leagues, through Venezuela and other adventures, was our first-base coach, and he gave me a big hug. My son Petey, fifteen years old, came running out in a Reds uniform with number 14 on the back. Teammates, Padres players, coaches—they all came by to congratulate me.

There were fireworks, a six-minute standing ovation from the crowd of 47,237 at Riverfront Stadium, and some kind of combination of joy and pride and relief and sadness (about my dad not being there with me to see this) came over me. It was the second time in my whole life that I'd ever cried, and these were hot tears that felt good. All I could think of was my dad. I looked up and saw him sitting there in a front-row box seat, not exactly smiling, because a game was still on, and my dad would want me to be thinking about my next hit, and the one after that, but looking proud and looking satisfied. Right behind him I saw Ty Cobb, and he didn't look real happy about this turn of affairs, but there wasn't a lot he could do about it.

The crowd chanted, "Pete, Pete," someone drove a Red Corvette onto the field as a gift from Chevrolet, its plates reading PR 4192, and Reds owner Marge Schott came out and I hugged her, too.

I thought of Red Grothaus, who, like my dad, had passed away too early to see this moment, and Uncle Buddy, and so many others, but mostly I kept thinking of my dad. It felt like he could rest a little easier, now that this was out of the way, and so could I.

I even got a call from President Ronald Reagan, who once made a living as a baseball announcer.

"If you'd been here tonight, you'd know why we think this is the baseball capital of the world right here in Cincinnati, Ohio," I told the president.

"Congratulations," he said. "You really have given a lift to the whole country."

CHAPTER 25

I Blew It, I Know That

Here's one thing I can say for sure: I don't think if my father had been alive, I'd have ever bet on baseball. I really don't. Not that I didn't gamble when my dad was alive—that was part of the world of sports I grew up with. Everybody bet on sports. But it's one thing to put down a few bucks on a game with a friend and another to place an illegal bet through a bookmaker. My dad would never have bet like that. Even when I was a full-grown man, playing the game of baseball, I was always very leery of what my dad would think about what I was doing, and I knew that I let my betting get to a point where it wouldn't have set well with him at all. Maybe the hunger I felt that drove me on the field also hurt me at times.

My dad was tough in so many ways, but he was a straight arrow. He didn't do bad things, and he didn't expect his kids to do bad things. He would have been ashamed of what I did. That's what matters to me more than anything, thinking about letting down my father. All he ever asked is that I give my all to make myself better and put everything I have into competing at the highest level and winning and excelling. In so many ways, I answered that call to action, but I didn't answer it in every way. I was a long, long way from perfect. I fell short. I messed up. I left a tarnish on my baseball career, on my legacy, and on the name Pete Rose—his name, too, and my son's name, and I will carry the pain of knowing what I've done for as long as I live.

I don't think betting is morally wrong. I don't even think betting on baseball is morally wrong. It's how you do it that matters. There are legal ways, and there are illegal ways, and betting on baseball the way I did was against the rules of baseball. What I did was wrong. But put it this way: If you're a jockey riding number two in the Kentucky Derby, then shouldn't you be betting on number two to win the Derby? Shouldn't you believe in that horse and believe in yourself? Shouldn't you put everything on the line and give your all to win?

Every night I always bet on my team to win. Did I ever bet against my team? Hell no. I hated to lose more than any man ever born. I went to battle every day and put everything I had into winning. I'm sorry that I let the fans down by betting on baseball and being banned. I'm not a man who goes around saying sorry, but on this one, I'm truly sorry, and I'm humbled by a sense of acceptance that came over me. I take the good with the bad, and mostly I love everything about my years in baseball. This is the stain that will always be there, and I can't wash it out, no matter what I do.

I know that if I ever make the Hall of Fame in some way, it's sure to be long after I'm gone from this world, and one thing baseball taught me long ago was to not worry about things you have no control over. That's beyond me. But I want you to know how I loved baseball, and that I lived a life dedicated to the sport, and played the game the way it should be played. It wasn't always pretty, but it was always all out. I believed in baseball as a test of will and a test of character, and I still do.

CHAPTER 26

Pete Jr. Makes the Big Leagues

always had a close bond with my firstborn son, Pete Rose Jr., born in 1969. When I got the phone call in November 1973 informing me that I'd been named National League MVP, Petey was only four years old, but he might have been more excited about the news than me and his mom, Karolyn. He was jumping up and down.

"Me and Daddy," he kept shouting with a grin. "We got the MVP."

I said at the time: "He probably did have a lot to do with me winning it. When he's there I want to excel and he comes to almost every home game. It was the same with my father. When he was there I wanted to do my best, maybe pushed myself that much harder."

Because of my strong bond with my dad, because of the way we were almost extensions of each other—with me being basically a copy of him in so many ways—it felt natural to me to have a son who wanted to be like me. Petey was always around me, just like I'd always been around my dad. He was a batboy like I'd been a batboy, except in his case he was a batboy for the Cincinnati Reds and Philadelphia Phillies. We talked about baseball all the time, like my dad and I had talked baseball. Petey hung out with other sons of major-leaguers, like Eduardo Perez in Cincinnati and Bret Boone and Aaron Boone in Philadelphia. Petey was always in the public eye, as New York sportswriter Dick Young found out when he wrote about Petey in July 1978.

"Pete Rose Jr. is eight," he wrote. "He's a national institution. He has his own tailor-made Reds uniform, with ROSE across the back shoulders and number 14 beneath it, just like the old man. He pounds his fist into the pocket of his glove incessantly and spits into it. He swings the bat from both sides. Ask him to give an imitation of Pete Rose at bat, and he'll go into the same tilted crouch, peek up ferociously from under the peak of the cap and snarl, 'Get that crap over the plate.' Since he was four years old, he has been breaking up people with 'Get that crap over the plate.'"

There was even a baseball card that came out in 1982 featuring me and my son, "Pete & Re-Pete; Pete Rose and son." He'd become Re-Pete just like they called me Re-Pete when I was a boy. I spent my whole life trying to live up to the example set by my father, who left some mighty big shoes to fill, and I guess for Petey I was also probably a hard act to follow.

Petey was drafted by the Baltimore Orioles and, like me, was sent to play in the New York–Penn League, only he played in Erie (and hit .276), not Geneva (where I hit .277), and later he played in the Sally League, as I had. By 1997 he was playing Double-A ball in the Reds organization, hitting over .300 for the Chattanooga Lookouts and closing in on 100 RBIs for the season.

We all thought it was finally his time to get a call-up. He'd batted .225 for Triple-A Indianapolis at the start of the season before being sent to Chattanooga, but he was making a strong case for himself. He and I talked twice a week and every time he played, he'd trace my career hits total of 4,256 in the infield dirt as a tribute to me.

That August 24, *The Atlanta Journal-Constitution* noted Petey was hitting .309 with twenty-one homers, and added: "Should be good enough, after nine seasons in the minors, to earn him a September promotion to Cincinnati, where he dreams of using his dad's old locker."

But nothing happened—and then came crushing news: REDS SWING AND MISS WITH ROSE JR. was the *Cincinnati Enquirer* headline that August 26.

"She was going to hire buses," wrote columnist Paul Daugherty. "This would be best, Karolyn Rose thought. Fill up two or three buses with friends from Delhi and Western Hills and Cheviot. Load them with the people who had followed her son's baseball career from Knothole to now. Bring them all in for . . . her son Pete's first as a Cincinnati Red."

But Jim Bowden, the Reds' GM at the time, announced that week the team would not be promoting Petey to the Reds when rosters expanded in September, even though at that point he'd homered in four straight games. In making the announcement, Bowden said he thought Aaron Boone, another third baseman in the Reds' system, was a better prospect. He claimed it would cost too much money to bring up Petey.

Columnist Paul Daugherty summed it up: "Thirty-thousand dollars. Too much to promote a Rose in Cincinnati."

He went on: "The Reds have made a nice effort of reaching out to their fans in the last year. They are trying to show that somewhere beyond the strikes, the greed, and the stupidity, baseball still has a heart. . . . So maybe once, you forget about who was drafted higher, who got more bonus money, who is a product of your farm system. One time, you wink at objectivity. You embrace a kid who's good for the game, who owns a regal pedigree, and who, frankly, would account for a whole lot more revenue than the $30,000 Bowden said it would cost to bring him here. And he's hitting .316 with power."

The *Enquirer* had its finger on the pulse of how fans and the people of Cincinnati were feeling about the whole issue, but they couldn't say the full truth, which probably everyone understood: My son was being punished for the sins of the father.

It had been eight years since I'd been banned from baseball by commissioner Bart Giamatti in 1989 for betting on baseball. Bart and I understood each other, and if he hadn't died suddenly, I'll always believe the two of us could have worked something out and I'd have been returned to my rightful place in the game. I deserved punishment. But keeping me from the game I loved my whole life— the game that *was* my life—now that was a mighty severe punishment. Not only was I being treated as some kind of outcast, so was my first-born son—and I was pissed off. I went on radio that week and told them I was advising Petey to retire from baseball after that season if he couldn't be treated fairly. He'd done the work and put up the numbers to deserve a look, and that's all anyone expected, a fair look.

Petey had stuck it out for nine years in the minor leagues, long after most everyone assumed he'd never get a shot at the big leagues. He was persistent. To be honest with you, he never got a fair chance. I hurt his career more than anything. When he was playing in the minor leagues, I had gotten suspended, the whole thing became a major controversy in baseball, and people took it out on him. People could be cruel. I wasn't going to the ballpark then, so they didn't know where I was, but he was easy to find. People would show up and wave five-dollar bills at him and taunt him. It was hard on Petey. He came through all that, proved with his bat that he belonged, and now he was having the door slammed in his face yet again. I was sure it was all because of me.

Then the Reds flip-flopped. They responded to the outcry against treating my son so unfairly—and of course it was huge news in Cincinnati. ROSE'S RISE IS CHEERED was the big headline in the *Enquirer*, and the paper ran a special info box with news on getting tickets "to see Pete Jr.," because everyone knew it was going to be a hot ticket.

"The response has been astronomical," Bowden said. "It has been, by far, the most overwhelming response from Reds' ticketholders during my five-year stay about anything."

"It's what I've wanted to do since I was a kid, and it's a feeling you can't describe," Petey told the papers.

His old friend Eduardo Perez said, "He'll get respect from the players here for what he has accomplished this year. I got a chill when they told me about it, and I'll get a chill seeing him out there. It's gonna be nerve-racking his first game, but he is the kind of kid who has always been in the spotlight all his life and used to it."

I was in the Bahamas and made arrangements to get back for the game. I was so proud of my son. On Labor Day, I was there in the stands to watch along with a crowd of more than 31,000 as Petey singled his second time up to earn a long ovation. It was an emotional day. Later he added a walk, so he went 1 for 3 for the day. The crowd was all there to see Petey, a big jump from what the Reds were drawing at the time. The next day, just to give you a comparison, attendance was 15,288, less than half of what it had been for Petey's well-publicized debut. Instead of costing the team thirty grand, calling Petey up made the team at least that much.

But they never really gave Petey a chance after that. He wasn't in the starting lineup the next day, which might have been manager Jack McKeon's decision, but probably not, so I'm not going to hold that against Trader Jack. The next day he decided to use Petey as a pinch hitter and sprung it on him.

"Get a bat and hit, Pete," Jack told him.

They didn't even give him time to warm up. To this day I'll never understand that. He'd put up the numbers to deserve a chance, the city was behind him, fans were energized—and they were busy with some private agenda. Is there something wrong with having a Pete Rose in your organization?

But as frustrating as all the front-office politics were, I'll never forget how wonderful it was to see my son play in the big leagues for the first time, wearing number 14. It felt like my dad was there in the stadium, the three of us joined together in a kind of chain.

Baseball Has to Make a Few Changes

I was raised to love sports and I'll love sports till the day I die, especially baseball. I didn't sour on baseball when I was banned from the sport and I didn't get turned off to watching baseball when my effort to be reinstated fell short. The game is the game. If you love baseball—and I don't think anyone loves baseball more than I do—then you're always going to enjoy watching it played, and I mean anywhere, from a sandlot in the North Pole to one in Key West. But it's getting harder and harder for me to watch Major League Baseball. The fun has drained out of it for me. And if it's getting more difficult for me to watch baseball, it's got to be more difficult for a lot of fans. The powers that be in baseball had better pay attention.

To me baseball looks like a sport trying to turn itself into a video game. I grew up listening to my favorite broadcasters painting pictures with words, bringing alive a whole world of detail. Nowadays about all they have to say is "Swing and a miss" and "Popped up!" and "That's a home run!" That's just plain boring! It's like the owners got together and tried to compress an entire game down into a few seconds of action; one three-run bomb in the third decides the game and everything else is a whole lot of garbage time. That might work great for the ESPN highlight hour, but how are you going to hold the attention of a new generation of young fans learning the game pitch by pitch if there's no strategy, no subtlety, no nuance?

Look, I started out in life with probably less natural talent than most big leaguers. I wasn't even the best player on my high school baseball team, and I turned myself into the all-time Hit King. How did I do that? Through hard work, of course, but also through becoming a close student of the art of hitting. I broke down every nuance I could, every little detail.

I was raised on baseball, and trained early to respect all its quirks and complexities. My dad talked to me constantly about how to watch a baseball game, what to notice, what to tune into and try to emulate. Above all, my dad didn't tolerate mental errors. One of the worst things I see in baseball now is a guy loses a ball in the sun and he's got his sunglasses up on top of his hat! That drives me crazy. I saw a guy in San Francisco lose a ball in the sun at his home ballpark. You don't know your own ballpark? Those are mistakes you can't tolerate as a manager and shouldn't tolerate as a fan.

Some call me one of the greatest students of hitting ever, up there with Ted Williams and Hank Aaron. I'll leave that to others to say, but we can agree: I've made it my life's work to understand everything that goes into making a baseball game play out the way it does. And I hardly recognize what I see out there now as baseball.

The explosion of home runs is ridiculous. I've seen so many home runs hit to the opposite field in recent years, I can't even believe it. Bryce Harper broke his bat in half in New York early in the 2018 season and still hit a 406-foot homer to center field off Jacob deGrom. Are you kidding me? That doesn't happen. Later that season, I saw a pop fly come down behind the dugout in Anaheim and—boing!—it bounced all the way up into the second deck! And you want to tell me the ball isn't juiced? Of course something is going on with the ball. You can't blame the players for that. That's the owners.

I never thought I'd get up on a cardboard box and start defending pitchers, but here I am: The poor guys can't catch a break! All the new ballparks are like bandboxes. Umpires won't call strikes. The ball travels like it's a Titleist. Everything is in favor of the hitter. I guess that's the way the owners want it.

They've proven to players that if you hit twenty-five to thirty-five home runs in a season, you can bet your ass you're going to land a contract paying you at least $10 million a year. So they all drop their back shoulders to elevate and try to hit home runs. Why should they care if they strike out all the time? They're not going to be judged on that.

I don't pretend to understand half of this analytical stuff they're always talking about now. Like when they say WAR (Wins Above Replacement), who is that "replacement"? If you want to compare me to the next guy, that I get. But how do you compare me to a figment of your imagination? How do you claim that means something? Sometimes it seems like the smart guys they're hiring from all these fancy colleges nowadays cooked up all this stuff to confuse people and give the owners a free hand in doing whatever the hell they want. Fans used to hold teams more accountable. They paid close attention and they knew who was good and who wasn't, who was playing all out and who wasn't.

When I was coming up in baseball, there were eight teams in the National League and eight teams in the American League, and in a lot of the country, baseball was the top sport, which meant that it could attract its share of the best high school and college athletes. Now there are thirty teams and brisk competition from other sports, like Major League Soccer and the National Hockey League.

There are only so many good athletes to go around, and the talent pool just isn't there for baseball to field thirty teams. As a result, players are promoted up through the farm system way too fast, and they never get a chance to learn the game right. If you don't spend much time in the minor leagues, or you don't spend time in a good college program, you're never going to master the fundamentals, and you're never going to get a chance to catch up. Baseball is not a game you can learn on the job. You ought to know how to play the game when you get to the big leagues, but that's usually not the case.

Like I said, I always took the attitude as a player that you might have a throw take off on you or you might drop a pop fly or make some other physical error, but you never wanted to make a mental error. In today's game there are more mental errors than there are physical errors, things like throwing to the wrong base or forgetting to back up a play or not knowing how many outs there are. More and more often you see guys who can't take care of the basics when they're hitting, like getting guys from second over to third, or getting them home from third.

That's why there are a lot of really bad teams in Major League Baseball now and, I hate to say it, a lot of bad players. You see it especially with the pitchers. With 30 teams in the majors compared to 16, you've got 140 pitchers in the big leagues now who wouldn't have been in the big leagues 50 years ago. But you also have 140 pitchers in Triple-A who wouldn't have been there—they'd have been in Double-A learning the ropes. But because of the need for arms, they get promoted before they're ready. There are great pitchers, your Kershaws and your Verlanders, but I can tell you I would love to be a hitter today.

So what should be done about the decline in the game? I wouldn't complain any if they decided to contract and go back to twenty-eight teams, or even less than that, but I'm not going to hold my breath. It would cost money to buy out the teams you're trying to contract, and I just don't see baseball owners wanting to pull out their wallets and fork over the dough that would take.

But here's a move that would be easy enough to make: Why not break the season into two halves and have winners for the first half, and winners for the second half, like they do in the minor leagues? I tell you, as a player, nothing is worse than hitting the All-Star break and already knowing you're on a team with no shot at postseason play. It's hard on the fans, too, when a team is dead in the water and going nowhere. They stay away in droves. But if you hit reset at the midpoint of the season and gave every team a new lease on life, the fans would be into the games again—and so would the players. A player—or a team—might have a terrible May but have a great August. It would mean no more trade deadline deals that tear apart a team—and their fans.

I'd also go over to shorter-term contracts for players. Now, that might not make me a popular man with current players, but I'm just thinking about the fans here and the quality of play they see on the field. Sparky Anderson once told me, "Give me twenty-five guys every year who go to spring training on the last year of their contract, and I'll go to the World Series every year." Those are guys who are always playing hungry. Those are guys who are going to bust their butts to give it their all. Sure, you can give a special player like Derek Jeter a hundred-year contract and he'd play just as hard every year, even if he were ninety years old, but it's just human nature that some guys, if you give them a long-term contract, are going to slack off and take extra days off and coast. That turns off the fans.

If the fans know you're giving it everything you've got, every single day, that buys a lot of loyalty. There has to be a way to have a limited number of multiyear contracts and make sure that the majority of players are on a shorter contract that will give them plenty of incentive to keep showing up and keep playing hard. In my era, I had to fight every year for the numbers to get a good contract. I had to fight every day, always busting my butt, even if it was the All-Star Game.

Home-run fever isn't getting the job done for baseball. Attendance keeps dropping. Every season from 2012 to 2018, total Major League Baseball attendance declined. Average attendance in 2016 was 30,131. The next year it dropped under 30,000—at 29,908—for the first time since 2003. Then in 2018 it slipped under 29,000.

If you remind people of what worked a generation or two ago to pull in fans, they accuse you of living in the past and being an old fogey. Let the accusations come—I've heard worse. Maybe we can't go back to the days when baseball was the national pastime, numero uno in the hearts and imaginations of fans, but we could try doing without all the bells and whistles and noise. When my dad would take me to see the Dodgers at Crosley Field and we'd sit right behind the dugout, every minute of the game had an electricity to it because you could yell something to Pee Wee Reese or Roy Campanella and you knew they'd hear you. You knew they might even say something back to you! It was like all the players and all the fans were connected.

I will never understand why so many teams nowadays work so hard at their noisy new ballparks to distract fans from paying attention to the game—or talking to each other. I grew up talking constantly about everything that happened at any game I attended, arguing about what we just saw or turning over every fine point of the game every which way. Now the loud music kicks in the instant the third out is made and no one can talk to anyone without shouting. They want the fans to feel entertained, I get it, but maybe this thing called baseball can entertain them. Maybe if you loosen up on some of these rule changes and let players be players, going in hard to second base and arguing with each other and the umps, that would be entertaining for people.

I know this: The way I played, I'd have been kicked out of every game by the fourth or fifth inning under today's rules. And fans loved that about me. They knew I cared. They didn't think I was out in right field wishing I could call my stockbroker to check on my portfolio. They knew I lived and breathed baseball, just the way they did, just the way my dad did. I don't know how you get that passion back, that fire, like nothing else matters. I know it starts with fathers and sons, mothers and sons, fathers and mothers and daughters, talking about a baseball game like something is at stake, like something is learned about character and commitment every time out there. There's a world of difference between that and seeing a sporting event as just one more slice of entertainment in a kid's day jammed full of them.

If this book accomplishes anything, I'd love to see it inspire a few conversations, maybe some fans old enough to have watched me play talking to younger people about how it made them feel, seeing me bust my butt day after day. I hope I made people feel good. I dedicated this book to the fans, because it was always all about you, living up to the standards my dad set for me every game so I knew I was giving the fans all the excitement and color and intensity they were hoping to see.

We all know baseball needs more of that now—more raw emotion, more giving a damn. The postseason is great, who doesn't love watching the World Series, but too many months of the season pass by without getting people really fired up. I don't know how you get back that kind of excitement that baseball generated nationally in the Big Red Machine days, but I know you'd better try or baseball is going to continue to lose its share of the American pie. It's the greatest game because it's America, open and unpredictable and all about putting a group of strangers together and having them work together as one. The passion to do that can't only be about a paycheck. It can't only be about winning a World Series. It has to be about playing the game right, every single game from spring training to the World Series, because doing a thing right is its own reward.

ACKNOWLEDGMENTS

I want to thank all the fans who come out to see me in Las Vegas. It's work, signing all day, but I love meeting people from all over the country and talking baseball with them. For information about events, corporate appearances, and autograph signings, contact my agent Ryan Fiterman of Fiterman Sports at ryan@fitermansports.com.

I was so focused all those years on giving baseball my all, I never went on a real vacation. Can you believe it? My dad never took the family on a vacation—unless you count our one annual excursion to Madison, Indiana, for the annual Madison Regatta, where we'd watch big hydroplane boats racing on the Ohio River—and I never had time for vacations in all the years since.

Finally, just recently, in my seventies, I went on my first real vacation. A buddy opened up a resort in Cabo San Lucas and I went down there with my fiancée, Kathy, and her son and daughter, Ashton and Cassandra, who both love golf. I've taken trips all over the world, but I was always working some of the time. When I went to Cabo with Kathy and her two kids, I didn't do anything work related, I just stayed at the resort and caddied for the kids playing golf. Now we go two times a year. Kathy is fun to be around. I love spending time with her. She's hilarious. I want to thank her for making me want to write this book and tell my story to a whole new generation.

Finally, I'd like to thank Christopher Richards, my editor on the project. I knew from our first meeting in New York that he got me, and at every step in the process, he was like a catcher calling a great game. Thanks also to the whole Penguin Random House marketing team. Steve Kettmann, a former baseball writer who is now codirector of a writers' retreat center in Northern California, helped me a lot, too.

PHOTOGRAPH CREDITS

Insert page 1: Bettmann / Getty Images

Insert page 2 (top and bottom): Bettmann / Getty Images

Insert page 3: David Durochik / AP Photo

Insert page 4: ZUMA Press, Inc. / Alamy Stock Photo

Insert page 5 (top): Bettmann / Getty Images

Insert page 5 (bottom): National Baseball Hall of Fame and Museum

Insert page 6: Bettmann / Getty Images

Insert page 7 (top): Bettmann / Getty Images

Insert page 7 (bottom): ZUMA Press, Inc. / Alamy Stock Photo

Insert page 8: Marty Lederhandler / AP Photo

Insert page 9: Harry Cabluck / AP Photo

Insert page 10: Marty Lederhandler / AP Photo

Insert page 11: Bob Daugherty / AP Photo

Insert page 12: U.S. National Archives and Records Administration / Jimmy Carter Library

Insert page 13: Bettmann / Getty Images

Insert page 14: National Baseball Hall of Fame and Museum

Insert page 15 (top): Aaron M. Conway

Insert page 15 (bottom): Jeff Goode / *Toronto Star* / Getty Images

Insert page 16: John Minchillo / AP Photo

INDEX

Printed in the United States
by Baker & Taylor Publisher Services